Historical American Biographies

P. T. BARNUM

Genius of the Three-Ring Circus

Karen Clemens Warrick

Enslow Publishers, Inc.

40 Industrial Road   PO Box 38
Box 398   Aldershot
Berkeley Heights, NJ 07922   Hants GU12 6BP
USA   UK

http://www.enslow.com

Library of Congress Cataloging-in-Publication Data

Warrick, Karen Clemens.
P.T. Barnum : genius of the three-ring circus / Karen Clemens Warrick.
    p. cm. — (Historical American biographies)
Includes bibliographical references (p.) and index.
ISBN 0-7660-1447-9
1. Barnum, P.T. (Phineas Taylor), 1810–1891—Juvenile literature.
2. Circus owners—United States—Biography—Juvenile literature. [1. Barnum,
P.T. (Phineas Taylor), 1810–1891. 2. Circus owners.] I. Title. II. Title: Genius of
the three-ring circus. III. Series.
 GV1811.B3W36 2001
791.3'092—dc21
[B]
                                                    00-010310

Printed in the United States of America

10 9 8 7 6 5 4 3 2

To Our Readers: We have done our best to make sure all Internet addresses in
this book were active and appropriate when we went to press. However, the
author and the publisher have no control over and assume no liability for the
material available on those Internet sites or on other Web sites they may link to.
Any comments or suggestions can be sent by e-mail to comments@enslow.com or
to the address on the back cover.

Illustration Credits: Circus World Museum, Baraboo, Wisconsin, pp. 7,
12, 99; Courtesy, American Antiquarian Society, pp. 15, 16, 36, 39, 45,
50, 61, 65, 71, 81, 83, 91, 93, 106; Enslow Publishers, Inc., pp. 52, 68,
78, 100; Historical Collections, Barnum Museum, p. 57; Historical
Collections, Bridgeport Public Library, pp. 27, 114; Karen Clemens
Warrick, p. 109.

Cover Illustrations: Courtesy, American Antiquarian Society (Inset);
Library of Congress (Background).

CONTENTS

Acknowledgments   4

1 Barnum's Jumbo Attraction . . .   5

2 Birth of a Humbug 14

3 Tricks of the Trade 23

4 The American Museum 33

5 General Tom Thumb 42

6 Husband and Father 54

7 Respect for a Humbug 63

8 Rebuilding Dreams 75

9 Under the Big Top 86

10 The Greatest Show
   on Earth 98

11 The World's Greatest
   Showman 108

Chronology 116

Chapter Notes 118

Glossary 124

Further Reading and
Internet Addresses 125

Index 126

Acknowledgments

Special thanks to all the members of my critique group—Abe, Arlene, Carolyn, Debra, Karyl, and Mary—who helped me capture the character of P. T. Barnum; and to Marilyn and her family, who made it possible for me to tour Bridgeport, Connecticut, the showman's hometown.

1

BARNUM'S JUMBO ATTRACTION

Ladies and gentlemen! Now presenting the stupendous, the incredible, the unbelievable, and altogether true tale of how Jumbo, the most renowned of all circus elephants, joined the star-studded cast of the Barnum's and London 7 United Monster Shows. Please direct your attention to the center ring, where this amazing story, joyous and tragic, is about to be told.

For twenty years, an enormous elephant had been a favorite attraction at the London Zoo. It stood ten feet nine inches high and weighed six tons. Hundreds of thousands of children had taken rides on its back. Its name was Jumbo, a variation of the African word *jamba*, which means elephant.

From across the Atlantic Ocean, P. T. Barnum, the world's greatest showman, eagerly eyed the enormous creature. He wanted Jumbo for his circus.

Jumbo's Double Definition

When an elephant was acquired by the Royal Zoological Gardens in London, the owners named the baby Jumbo. Jumbo was a rather undersized baby. Matthew Scott, his keeper, nursed and coddled Jumbo until he grew to larger-than-average size.

The elephant's huge frame, and P. T. Barnum's dramatic advertising of his circus star, soon added a new meaning to the word *jumbo*. The word was adopted into American English and used to describe something of enormous size.

Though he had "no hope of ever getting possession of him," Barnum offered ten thousand dollars to the London Zoo.[1] However, in 1881, when Jumbo began to throw temper tantrums in his quarters, the London Zoo decided to accept Barnum's offer. The zoo feared the huge beast might harm his keeper or possibly some of the children who came to see him.

Barnum was overjoyed with his purchase, but he was not content to simply pack up his new circus star and quietly sail for home.[2] First, the circus owner wanted to convince the American public of Jumbo's extraordinary worth. To do this, Barnum decided to persuade the English that they were being tricked out of a national treasure. A London newspaper helped him plant the seed. "No more quiet garden strolls, no shady trees, green lawns, and flowery thickets," London's

When Jumbo posed with his trainer, Matthew Scott, his size was often exaggerated. A reporter said in March 1883, "His trunk is the size of an adult crocodile, his tail is as big as a cow's leg, and he made footprints in the sands of time resembling an indentation as if a very fat man had fallen off a very high building."

Daily Telegraph printed in protest: "Our amiable monster must dwell in a tent, take part in the routine of a circus, and, instead of his by-gone friendly trots with British girls and boys, and perpetual luncheon on buns and oranges, must amuse a Yankee mob, and put up with peanuts and waffles."[3]

British citizens were outraged. Parliament (Great Britain's lawmaking body) and Queen Victoria practically

begged Barnum to cancel the deal. Lawsuits were brought against the zoo officers for making the sale. Barnum's agent was threatened with imprisonment if force of any kind were used on Jumbo when he was moved. Barnum received hundreds of letters asking him to reconsider. He was offered huge sums of money to cancel the sale.

Determined to have his Jumbo prize, Barnum refused to call off the transaction. Instead, he cabled the *Daily Telegraph*, saying that a "Hundred thousand pounds [British currency] would be no inducement to cancel purchase."[4]

A Jumbo Strike

Meanwhile, Barnum made arrangements for Jumbo's move across the Atlantic Ocean to join the circus. An enormous rolling cage was built of oak and iron. But when it came time for Jumbo to walk in, the elephant refused. Barnum's agents wired for instructions: "Jumbo is lying in the garden and will not stir. What shall we do?" Barnum answered: "Let him lie there a week if he wants to. It is the best advertisement in the world."[5]

Excitement mounted in the United States as daily accounts of Jumbo's sit-down strike filled the papers. Jumbo-mania swept across the country. Songs, poems, and Jumbo souvenirs appeared by the thousands before a solution was found. Finally, Matthew Scott, Jumbo's keeper, agreed to accompany the elephant to the United States. With Scott leading the way, Jumbo walked into the six-ton box, and Barnum could write, "Jumbo was mine."[6]

It took sixteen horses to move the cage, and thousands of people followed. Scott remembered, "the grief of the children was really sorrowful."[7] The twelve tons of cargo—the combined weight of Jumbo and his cage—were loaded aboard the *Assyrian Monarch*. For his last meal in England, Jumbo dined on fruit and bonbons while grieving lords and ladies attended a good-bye dinner on the ship.

The cost of shipping the elephant to the United States was only a thousand dollars at that time. However, Barnum had to pay for fifty tons of freight as well as the fares of the two hundred America-bound immigrants that the elephant displaced.

Jumbo's American Debut

The ship arrived in New York on Easter, 1882. Jumbo was welcomed by thousands of New Yorkers. The crowd formed a parade behind the rolling cage as Jumbo was led to the Hippodrome building, now the site of Madison Square Garden, where the circus was about to open. During Jumbo's first three weeks in the United States, the circus's daily ticket sales were never less than $4,797.65, with the highest amount— $14,443.26—collected on April 28, 1882. Though the large crowds cannot be credited to Jumbo alone, the publicity stirred by his purchase certainly helped boost ticket sales.

The elephant joined the menagerie, a cast of wild animals, which was already part of the Barnum's and

London Circus. The three-ring circus was already home to thirty-two camels, eight giant baboons, six trained kangaroos, and thirty other elephants. However, Jumbo was the largest and now the most famous. Advertised as "The Towering Monarch of his Mighty Race, Whose Like the World Would Never See Again," Jumbo quickly became the pride of the circus. He always marched in the procession at the beginning of a performance around the circus's three rings with a baby elephant, named Bridgeport, to emphasize his astonishing size.

In four short seasons, Jumbo achieved unheard of success as he traveled the country in his own special train car. He was loved by millions of American children and adults. Jumbo became the most famous animal in the world—perhaps the most celebrated in history. The elephant was Barnum's pride and joy, his favorite of all the extraordinary creatures in a long career.[8]

A Giant Derailed

On the night of September 15, 1885, tragedy struck as the circus ended its final performance in St. Thomas, Ontario, Canada. Twenty-nine elephants had already finished their routines and had been led down the railroad tracks to their waiting cars. Only the smallest—Tom Thumb—and the largest—Jumbo—had remained for the show's grand finale.

As keeper Matthew Scott guided the two elephants along the railroad tracks, he heard a whistle, but the warning came too late. An unscheduled

Monstrous Temper Tantrums

Jumbo never again showed the temper that had cost him his home at the London Zoo. He adapted well to circus life and especially enjoyed the bottle of beer that Matthew Scott, his trainer, shared with him at bedtime. This fact led Barnum to consider selling a special Jumbo-shaped beer mug.

express train hit Tom Thumb first, scooping him up, then knocking him down a steep embankment. Jumbo tried to run, but the circus train, sitting on a sidetrack, blocked his only escape route. The elephant was struck from behind. The locomotive derailed. Jumbo was crushed. His skull was broken in more than a hundred places. The dying elephant was comforted in his final moments by his trainer. It took one hundred sixty men to drag the immense elephant's body off the tracks. Scott was overwhelmed by the loss of his old friend.

Barnum, too, was disheartened by this enormous loss.[9] However, he was not about to let the tragedy defeat him. The showman had a plan to keep Jumbo's memory alive. Within forty-eight hours, a taxidermist—someone who stuffs and mounts animal skins—named Henry A. Ward went to work. With two assistants, Ward first measured every dimension of Barnum's superstar. Then, with the help of six local butchers,

"JUMBO"
After fatal accident, September 15th, 1885
St. Thomas, Ontario,
Canada.

A crowd gathered around the body of Barnum's jumbo star. Circus
and railroad officials blamed each other for the accident.

the taxidermist removed the elephant's 1,538-pound
hide and collected 2,400 pounds of bone.

Ward received only twelve hundred dollars for the
task and complained bitterly in letters to Barnum, but
he did the job. (Today, a taxidermist would charge
more to stuff and mount a deer.) When the circus
opened in April 1886, spectators were treated to double Jumbos—one made of the elephant's hide, the
other of its skeleton.

Both mammoth models were mounted on special
spring wagons and pulled along in the circus's grand

parade during the following season. Alice, another London Zoo elephant, was trained to play Jumbo's grieving widow, and a long line of the circus's regular elephants played her attendants. All had been trained to carry black-bordered sheets with their trunks and wipe their eyes every few steps. Jumbo would never be forgotten, thanks to the efforts of the great American showman, P. T. Barnum.

And now ladies and gentlemen, on with the main event, the truly amazing story of the circus owner who brought Jumbo to the United States, the man known as America's Greatest Showman and America's Greatest Humbug, the one, the only, Phineas Taylor Barnum.

2

BIRTH OF A HUMBUG

Phineas Taylor Barnum always regretted not being born on the Fourth of July. He arrived one day late, on July 5, 1810.[1] He was born in a two-story frame house in Bethel, Connecticut, a rural community near Danbury, in the foothills of the Berkshire and the Taconic mountains.

Taylor, as his family called him, was the first child of Philo Barnum and his second wife, Irena Taylor. Philo Barnum had already had five children with Polly Fairchild, who had died in 1808. Philo married Irena within six months of his first wife's death, possibly to provide a mother for his children. He had five more children with Irena—Taylor, son Eder, and three girls—Mary, Cordelia, and Almira.

Phineas Taylor Barnum was born in this house on Elm Street in Bethel, Connecticut.

Philo Barnum tried to make a living as farmer, tailor, tavern-keeper, and grocer. He ran a livery stable, renting out teams and carriages and tending travelers' horses overnight. He even operated a small freight business between Norwalk and Danbury. But he had little success at any of these jobs.

Taylor was named for Irena's father, Phineas Taylor, who had fought in the American Revolution and served in the Connecticut state legislature. The mop-headed, bespectacled, boisterous figure adored his grandson. He lavished all his attention on his

Phineas Taylor, Barnum's maternal grandfather, prided himself on staying a jump ahead of the next man with his practical jokes.

namesake, and was the first person Taylor clearly remembered.

Taylor recalled one of his grandfather's traits in particular. He later wrote that his strong-willed, crafty grandfather was a wag—a practical joker. He would "go farther, wait longer, work harder, . . . to carry out a practical joke, than for anything else under heaven."[2] In fact, Taylor was the victim of one of the most prolonged practical jokes Grandfather Taylor ever played.

A Rich Inheritance

The stage for this infamous practical joke was set during Taylor's christening. Grandfather Taylor gave his daughter's firstborn the deed to five acres of land known as Ivy Island. From the time Taylor was four until he turned ten years old, he was often reminded of this gift by his neighbors and family: "My grandfather always spoke of me (in my presence) to the neighbors and to strangers as the richest child in town,

A Humbug and a Wag

During Barnum's time, the word *humbug* could mean something done to cheat or deceive, or it could describe a person who was not what he claimed to be. A wag was a joker, or someone with a witty sense of humor.

In New England in the 1820s and 1830s, the practical joke was one of the few socially permissible forms of fun. Trickery was entertainment and a method of testing wits. Barnum claimed to take after his grandfather and appreciated practical joking. Putting one over on people, when it did no harm, added merriment and was part of what gave life its zest, Barnum believed.

since I owned the whole of 'Ivy Island,' one of the most valuable farms in the State."[3]

As Taylor heard more about his inheritance, he dreamed of growing up a respected and important man. He wanted to see this island, which was only about a half mile north of his home. Finally, when he was ten, his father agreed to let Taylor visit his property. Before he left home that morning, his mother cautioned him not to get so excited that he made himself sick or return home with a swollen head.

Barnum later recorded these details about this memorable excursion:

As we approached . . . we found the ground swampy and wet and were soon obliged to leap from bog to bog. A mis-step brought me up to my middle in water. . . . after floundering through the morass, I found myself half-drowned, hornet-stung, mud-covered, and out of breath, on . . . the margin of a stream.[4]

The hired man who had accompanied Taylor cut a small oak to bridge the flowing water, and finally he reached his island. Once there, Barnum remembered, "I saw nothing but a few stunted ivies and straggling trees. The truth flashed upon me. I had been the laughing-stock of the family and neighbors for years. My valuable Ivy Island was a worthless bit of barren land."[5] Taylor's rich inheritance consisted of about five acres of bogs and a few scrubby trees choked with the only kind of ivy to be found on the island—poison ivy.

When he returned home that evening, all the neighbors gathered with his grandfather and family to congratulate and tease him. Having spent ten years preparing this joke, the people of Bethel spent the next five laughing over it.

Boyhood in Puritan New England

The Barnums, like most families in the community of Bethel, were members of the Congregational Church. Taylor spent every Sunday sitting on the hard pews of the church's meetinghouse. Congregational doctrine preached that man, by nature, was wicked, and that, from the beginning of time, God had selected those who would and would not be saved. Good works could not save those who were destined to eternal hell. However, people were expected to work hard at being good anyway, to prove that they were among the chosen.

Barnum remembered leaving prayer meetings at the age of thirteen or fourteen, "in the fear of hell . . . I used to go home and pray and cry and beg God to take me out of existence if He would only save me."[6]

Amusement of most sorts was considered sinful. Shows and theater performances were forbidden by law. Colorful storytelling, quick wit, stretching the truth, and inventive practical jokes were the only allowable reliefs.

Grandfather Phineas Taylor was one of the few in the community who attended the Universalist Church. Its doctrine was not as harsh as the Congregational Church's. Universalists believed that all men and women of faith would be saved, not just a select few. Taylor eventually adopted his grandfather's religious beliefs.

Childhood and School Days

Taylor's life in Bethel was much like that of any young farm boy growing up in New England. He played tag and hide-and-seek with his friends. He fetched the cows, carried in firewood, shucked corn, and weeded, but he never really liked physical labor.[7]

Barnum later wrote that he "began to accumulate pennies and 'four-pences'" at an early age.[8] When he was six, his grandfather informed him that all his little pieces of coin amounted to one dollar. Together

they went to the village tavern, with Taylor's little handkerchief full of coins, and exchanged them all for a silver dollar. Barnum wrote,

> Never have I seen the time (nor shall I ever again) when I felt so rich, so absolutely independent of all the world, as I did when I looked at that monstrous big silver dollar, and felt that it was all my own. . . . I believed without the slightest reservation, that the entire earth and all its contents could be purchased by that wonderful piece of bullion, and that it would be a bad bargain at that.[9]

From that moment on, earning money became Taylor's obsession. He sold molasses candy and earned ten cents for a day of plowing or for scraping one hundred cow horns for a comb maker.

At age six, Taylor started school. He was unusually quick in mathematics and soon developed a talent for writing. Like most young boys, he was mischievous and often got into trouble. When hard swats from a ruler did not work, Taylor was banished to the "dungeon" in the school's basement. Later in life, Barnum complained that his father often kept him away from his studies to work on the farm or in the store. However, he seems to have attended school regularly enough to have mastered the basics.

To Work

Taylor disliked farm chores but was glad to work in his father's country store.[10] There, he learned lessons that would serve him later in life, such as how to haggle over a price, how to strike a hard bargain, and how to pull the wool over a purchaser's eyes, a practice accepted by New Englanders as part of being a good businessman.

He could soon spot farmers' short measurements—when the portions were not quite what the farmers claimed—and their wives' rag swindles—bundles of rags stuffed with worthless trash, stones, and ashes instead of scraps of cloth. Shrewdness was necessary in the country store, where payment was often made in butter, eggs, hats, and hickory nuts instead of with cash.

Barnum liked to illustrate the morality of business in those days with a story he often repeated. The story was about the owner of a village grocery who was also a church official. Once before breakfast, he shouted downstairs to his clerk:

> "John, have you watered the rum?"
> "Yes, sir."
> "And sanded the sugar?"
> "Yes, sir."
> "And dusted the pepper?"
> "Yes, sir."
> "And chicoried [added chicory root, a coffee substitute, to] the coffee?"
> "Yes, sir."
> "Then come up to prayers."[11]

These practices seem dishonest today, but at that time, they were part of the game. Both the owner and the customer hoped to strike the better bargain.

Suddenly, at the age of fifteen, Barnum's childhood was over. Philo Barnum became ill with a fever one day in March. He died six months later on September 7, 1825, at the age of forty-eight.

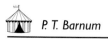

After the family business was sold and the debts paid off, the Barnum family was bankrupt. Barnum later wrote:

> The world looked dark indeed. . . . My mother was left with five children. I was the oldest, and the youngest was only seven years of age. We followed the remains of husband and parent to their resting-place and returned to our desolate home, feeling that we were forsaken by the world, and that but little hope existed for us this side the grave.[12]

Even the shoes he wore to his father's funeral had not been paid for: "I began the world with nothing, and was barefooted at that."[13]

3

TRICKS OF THE TRADE

To help support his family, Phineas Taylor Barnum took a job as a clerk in a general store in Grassy Plain, a settlement a mile outside of Bethel. He worked for his room and board and six dollars a month. Within the first few months, Barnum demonstrated that he had a head for business.

It all began when the young clerk traded for a wagonload of green glass bottles. The storeowner said that the bottles were a bad bargain. He thought it would take twenty years to sell them all. After assuring his boss that every bottle would be gone within three months, Barnum organized a lottery. One thousand tickets would be sold at fifty cents each. In return, Barnum promised to award five hundred prizes. The

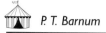

grand prize was twenty-five dollars, payable in any kind of goods the customer desired. The other 499 prizes, valued from twenty-five cents up to five dollars, consisted of items Barnum selected. The green glass and some old tin ware made up most of the prizes. For example, one five-dollar prize winner took away a pair of cotton hose, a cotton handkerchief, two tin cups, four one-pint glass bottles, three tin skimmers, a one-quart glass bottle, six tin nutmeg graters, and eleven half-pint glass bottles.[1] Tickets sold quickly. However, when the winners came to exchange tickets for prizes, they realized they had been hoaxed. Most laughed at the joke, then went off loaded down with baskets and bags full of the green glass and tin ware. Within ten days, every glass bottle and all the old tin ware had disappeared. The most appreciative witness of Barnum's lottery scheme was his grandfather, who proudly proclaimed the lad "a chip off the old block."[2]

Learning the Business

At sixteen, Barnum began clerking in a Brooklyn grocery near New York City. By watching the sales and noting prices at wholesale auctions, where grocers purchased quantities of teas, sugar, and molasses for resale, he learned to be a shrewd barterer. He was soon handling all the purchasing for the store.

Though he was good at his job, Barnum discovered that he preferred to earn a living through ventures in which he could sink or swim due to his own merit. So, the teenage entrepreneur (someone who takes the risk

Young Gambling Man

Lotteries were big business during this time. It was a well-accepted fact that people would gamble in lotteries for their own reward or to benefit a church in which the evils of gambling were condemned.

To make a success of his green bottle lottery, Barnum applied the experience he had gained between the ages of twelve and fifteen, running small neighborhood lotteries. The prizes for these youthful ventures were cakes, oranges, and molasses candy, with the highest prize worth about five dollars. Barnum usually earned a profit of 20 to 25 percent of the tickets sold.

of starting his or her own business with the hope of making a profit) quit the grocery to run his own saloon for six months. Then his grandfather offered Barnum half a house rent-free to start a business in Bethel, so he sold his business for a nice profit and returned home.

Now eighteen, Barnum divided his time between his Yellow Store, a fruit and confectionery business, and organizing lotteries. Once again, he studied the success of other lottery managers and soon had lottery offices throughout Connecticut.

Time away from his businesses was spent courting Charity Hallett. The two had met while Barnum was clerking in Grassy Plains. Charity bought bonnets from the hatmaker in whose home Barnum had boarded. During one of Charity's shopping trips, it began to storm. When she was afraid to ride home to Bethel

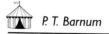

alone, Barnum agreed to escort her. Immediately attracted by the young woman's laugh and smile, Barnum wished the ride had been twenty miles instead of one, storm or no storm.[3]

Irena Barnum felt that her son could do better than a woman who earned her living by sewing for others. Barnum, however, was convinced that Charity was "one of the best women in the world."[4] Charity was a member of the Unitarian Church, educated, and a supporter of abolitionists, who called for an end to slavery. At this time, the number who supported abolition was small. Most were middle-class church members living in New England.

During the summer of 1829, nineteen-year-old Barnum proposed to twenty-one-year-old Charity Hallett. To avoid Irena Barnum's disapproval, Barnum and Hallett were married in New York City at the home of Charity's uncle on November 8. After the young couple returned to Bethel, three weeks passed before Irena Barnum invited her son and new daughter-in-law to spend the day with her.

Later, Barnum admitted that he was young for marriage. He added, however, that if he had waited twenty years longer, he "could not have found another woman so well suited to my disposition and so admirable and valuable in every character as a wife, a mother, and a friend."[5]

Religion and Politics

For the next few years, Barnum lived in Bethel with his wife. He sold everything from Bibles to brandy in

When Barnum married Charity Hallett in 1829, he described her as a "fair, rosy-cheeked, buxom-looking girl." This photograph shows Charity Barnum many years later.

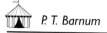

his Yellow Store, managed his lottery offices, and dabbled in real estate and book auctions. However, these ventures did not consume all his energy, and Barnum jumped into the religious and political controversies of the time. He began by writing articles criticizing the clergy-sponsored Blue Laws—laws that prohibited dancing, shows, sports, and businesses such as lotteries from operating on Sunday.

When the local newspaper refused to publish his writings, Barnum started his own weekly newspaper. The first issue of *The Herald of Freedom* appeared on October 19, 1831. Barnum's youthful enthusiasm soon got him into legal trouble.

After he printed an accusation he believed to be true—that a church deacon was guilty of "usury [charging too much interest] of an orphan boy"—the deacon took Barnum to court.[6] Barnum was convicted of libel, or printing something false and damaging. He was sentenced to sixty days in jail and fined one hundred dollars. Once again, Barnum made the best of his defeat. His jail cell, newly papered and carpeted, served as a meeting place for friends, and he kept editing his paper. When he was released, Barnum was escorted home by a parade of sixty carriages, forty horsemen, and a marching band.

A New Career

Caroline Cordelia, the Barnums' first daughter, was born on May 27, 1833. The next year, the Connecticut legislature banned lotteries, viewed as a form of gambling, ending Barnum's most reliable source of income.

Bored with the produce business, he sold the Yellow Store to friends and left his newspaper.[7] Then he moved his family to New York City to seek his fortune.

In New York, Barnum opened a boardinghouse and a grocery store. He made a fair profit, but was dissatisfied.[8] Every day the curly-haired young man with wide blue eyes and a large, round nose read the papers, which were filled with advertisements that he recognized as hoaxes. He studied how to profit by scamming the public. When the opportunity presented itself, Barnum took his first step toward a career as a showman. The venture involved Joice Heth, who claimed to be a 161-year-old slave. By her owner's account, she had cared for George Washington at his birth.

When Barnum learned that Heth's present owner wished to sell her, he caught the next stagecoach to Philadelphia to see the curiosity for himself. Joice Heth was a blind black slave. Her withered legs did not move. The fingernails on her left hand were four inches long. She weighed only forty-six pounds. Yet she talked almost incessantly about her "dear little George" and how she had not only been present at his birth but "raised" him.[9]

A crumbling bill of sale, for a black woman of fifty-four years named Joice Heth signed by Augustine Washington (George's father) and dated February 5, 1727, was offered as proof of her age. Feeling certain that Joice Heth was a potential gold mine, Barnum negotiated the asking price from three thousand down to one thousand dollars and purchased the right to exhibit Heth for a ten-month period.

By the fall of 1835, Barnum had his "astonishing curiosity" on display in New York.[10] Handbills and posters plastered the city. Two backlit Joice Heth transparencies, two by three feet in size, were displayed outside the exhibition hall where Barnum collected an average of fifteen hundred dollars a week. Crowds thronged to hear Joice Heth answer questions, sing hymns, and tell stories.

Although Barnum had no formal experience with showmanship, he had a sense of drama, a way with words, and an uncanny ability to take advantage of his opportunities. When the showman took Heth on tour through New England, where abolition sentiments were already high, Barnum did not advertise the fact that she was a slave. Instead, he invented a story in which he claimed that all the proceeds from Heth's exhibition went toward purchasing the freedom of her five great-grandchildren.

When ticket sales began to taper off in New York, Barnum penned an open letter to a newspaper signed, "A Visitor."[11] He charged that Heth was a fake, that she was "a curiously constructed automaton, made up of whalebone, India-rubber, and numberless springs," and that Levi Lyman, whose job was to introduce Heth and answer questions from the audience, was "a ventriloquist."[12] Again crowds gathered to see if this could possibly be true.

With this turn of events, the showman realized that the truth was not a necessity. In fact, he discovered that the public actually enjoyed being deceived, as long as they were also amused.[13] The hoax ended on February 19, 1836, when Joice Heth died.

Showman

Distrust of entertainers had come to the United States with the Puritans, a Protestant religious group with extremely strict beliefs. In the 1830s, many church members still believed it was a sin to go to the theater or other places of amusement. Plays were often suggestive. The audience was frequently drunk and disorderly. Fights were not unusual, both on and off the stage. The public distrusted people who made a living "playing" rather than working.

Those who preceded Barnum in show business had done little to change these attitudes. To be called a showman at this time was not a compliment. However, Barnum believed in and defended the educational value of his exhibitions. When the clergy in Lenox, Massachusetts, denounced circuses from the pulpit, Barnum made his way up the steps. He spoke out strongly against church policies that interfered with his freedom to amuse and be amused. Barnum fought this attitude all his life, but never really overcame it.

There is no doubt that Joice Heth was a hoax. Evidence from an autopsy indicated she was probably about 80 years old, not 161. However, with this successful exhibition, at age twenty-five P. T. Barnum was on his way to fame and fortune. "I had at last found my true vocation," he wrote.[14]

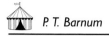

A Traveling Showman

In April, after Heth's death, Barnum sent Charity and their daughter back to Bethel while he toured with Aaron Turner's Old Columbian Circus, one of the first circuses in the United States to use tents. "The circus then had just nine horses and four wagons," remembered Hyatt Frost, who was a child at that time. "The bandsmen put up the tent and the performers made the ring. The artists dressed at the hotels and made a procession on horseback. Admission was twenty-five cents, children half price."[15]

With the money he earned, Barnum formed his own group of traveling performers and toured the South with a variety show, Barnum's Grand Scientific and Musical Theater. In May 1837, Barnum disbanded the show, returned to Bethel and his family, and looked for another way to advance his career.

THE
AMERICAN
MUSEUM

More than a quarter of a million people lived in New York in 1841 when Barnum moved his family back to the city. Many, too poor to buy their own homes, lived in boardinghouses. These boardinghouses lacked an important social outlet found in the traditional family home—the parlor, or living room. Young people and families entertained themselves with parlor games such as charades and checkers or sang songs around the piano. Boardinghouse residents had to look outside their homes for recreation.

They might choose to attend magic shows, puppet shows, hot-air balloon shows, art and science expositions, fairs, or lectures. The Puritans' influence was declining. However, many people still believed that

plays were suggestive and immoral, and respectable citizens were reluctant to be seen at theaters, no matter how elegant.

Of all the entertainments, museums were the least objectionable. Museum lecture rooms could present dramatic plays and variety acts disguised as educational programs. At this time, nearly every large city boasted at least one privately owned museum, such as John Scudder's American Museum in New York City.

In 1841, Barnum learned that the contents of the American Museum were up for sale. Barnum repeatedly visited the museum and knew the asking price of fifteen thousand dollars was well below the collection's worth. As a "thoughtful looker-on," he was soon convinced that "energy, tact, and liberality [broad-mindedness] were only needed to make it [the American Museum] a paying [profitable] institution."[1] Barnum believed this was the opportunity he had been looking for.

Though all Barnum's money was invested in his boardinghouse and grocery store, that did not stop the resourceful entrepreneur. After negotiating a sale price of twelve thousand dollars instead of the fifteen thousand being asked, Barnum approached the owner of the museum's building, Francis Olmsted, and convinced him to buy the collection on Barnum's behalf.

Impressed by Barnum, Olmsted agreed to make the purchase if Barnum could provide a piece of property as collateral—property that would become Olmsted's if Barnum did not make his payments. Everything Barnum owned was mortgaged, except for

Ivy Island, the five-acre gift from his grandfather. After a moment's hesitation, he offered Olmsted the parcel. It was accepted as security, sight unseen, and Barnum thought the deal was done.

Unfortunately, a group of speculators upset Barnum's plans, offering the full fifteen thousand for the museum's contents before Barnum's loan was settled. The New York Museum Company, as the group called itself, planned to issue and sell stock to cover the purchase price. Barnum, however, did not give up easily. He wrote letters to local newspapers, cautioning the public against buying the museum stock. When the stock's value dropped, the speculators lost their down payment, and Barnum secured the American Museum for himself.

Barnum moved Charity, Caroline, and baby Helen, who was born on April 18, 1841, into an apartment in the museum building. During the first year, the family lived on a budget of six hundred dollars a year, applying most of the museum's profits to paying off the loan or to renovations. Barnum wrote later that "my treasure of a wife" would have managed on a household budget of only four hundred dollars, if necessary, to help him repay his debt more quickly.[2]

Grand Promotion

The business of rebuilding the museum became the focus of Barnum's energies. The new owner developed a three-part plan. The first part required extensive renovations. Colorful world flags lined the roof and a huge revolving lighthouse lamp was installed, creating the city's first spotlight. The most dramatic change actually happened overnight. After weeks of secret preparations, Barnum's crew installed a series of large oval paintings between the nearly one hundred windows along the museum's upper stories—literally in one night. The paintings featured polar bears, elephants, ostriches, giraffes, tapirs, pelicans, kangaroos, and tigers. The effect was eye-catching. According to Barnum, it increased his revenues by one hundred dollars a day.

Barnum's renovated American Museum, located at the corner of Ann Street and Broadway in New York City. Notice the oval portraits of animals between the windows.

Barnum began to feature a multitude of live acts such as Chinese jugglers, snake charmers, rope dancers, a glassblower, and ventriloquists. One act that continually appeared on Barnum's stage was the giant or overweight child.

The museum held contests. Most successful of all were the baby shows. Prizes were awarded for categories such as finest baby, fattest baby, and the best sets of certifiable twins, triplets, and quadruplets.

Barnum was always searching for something new and different to offer his audiences. He arranged to share exhibits and acts with other museum owners such as his good friend, Moses Kimball of the Boston Museum.

All receipts not used to pay expenses and his debt to Olmsted went into the American Museum's advertising budget, the second part of Barnum's grand plan. He advertised aggressively and was constantly thinking up new ways to publicize the museum. He placed oversized banners on the outside of his building and hung illuminated transparencies that showed up at night. Barnum invented the country's first bulletin wagons—carts that were plastered with advertising posters and signs.

Barnum was always willing to try the outlandish, even the annoying, to bring notoriety to the museum. Once, he employed a man to march from corner to corner around the intersection in front of the museum. The first time around, the man laid a single brick on top of the sidewalk on each corner. During each successive round, he picked up each brick and replaced it with another. The man was instructed to pretend to be deaf and to pay no attention to those who might gather to watch him. At the end of each hour, he was to enter the American Museum and walk through the halls. Curious spectators often purchased tickets and followed the man inside. The bizarre spectacle continued for several days until the police complained that the crowds were blocking the sidewalks.

The third part of Barnum's plan was to build a reputation for the museum and for himself. Again, the showman was successful. Soon, New Yorkers were boasting about Barnum's American Museum in guidebooks. It quickly became a place all tourists planned to visit. In 1850, an Englishman stated that the museum owner would be remembered not for his exhibits, but because "[Barnum] represents the enterprise and energy of his countrymen in the 19th century, as [George] Washington represented their resistance to oppression in the century preceding."[3]

A New Hoax

In the spring of 1842, Barnum was approached by Moses Kimball of the Boston Museum. Kimball offered Barnum an embalmed mermaid bought near Calcutta, India, by a Boston sea captain in 1817. The captain had paid six thousand dollars for the object, a price that would equal about eighty thousand dollars today. Even on close examination, it was difficult to see how the object might have been fabricated, but Barnum certainly recognized it as a hoax. He and Kimball agreed to share the expenses and profits of

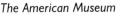
exhibiting this curiosity, which was supposedly captured off what are now called the Fiji Islands. They named it the Fejee Mermaid.

Once again, Barnum engineered a publicity campaign that made people wonder. He printed entertaining stories about the discovery of the mermaid near the Fejee Islands by the fictitious Dr. J. Griffin from London's Lyceum of Natural History. Griffin was, in fact, a colleague with whom Barnum often worked, named Levi Lyman. The story claimed that the English scientist would be in the United States with the Fejee Mermaid for a short while. Barnum distributed pamphlets and even managed to have three local newspapers print engravings of the curiosity. Excitement mounted

A CORRECT LIKENESS OF THE FEJEE MERMAID.
Reduced in size from Sunday Herald.

The "Fejee Mermaid" can be viewed today at the Barnum Museum in Bridgeport, Connecticut.

The Prince of Humbugs

Barnum insisted that the title "Prince of Humbugs" was a nickname he gave himself.[4] The term could be used for two opposite characters: "the outright swindler . . . [or Barnum's] own type of playful humbug, developed in order to increase . . . 'notoriety.'"[5]

During the early years of his career, Barnum was proud to be called the "prince of humbugs." He rationalized his trickery by insisting that he gave the paying customer more for his or her money than any other amusement establishment. In 1861, Barnum supposedly gave the following speech:

That Prince of Humbugs, BARNUM, so it appears
Some folks have designated me for several years—
Well, I don't murmur; indeed, when they embellish it,
To tell the truth, my friends I rather relish it.[6]

as New Yorkers waited for the mermaid's one-week exhibition.

The mermaid was eighteen inches long, black, and shriveled. The upper part of its body was hairy. The bottom part was a scaly tail that looked something like a mermaid's. Though many viewers were disappointed, the Fejee Mermaid drew large crowds. When the curiosity was moved from a concert hall, where it was exhibited for a week, to the American Museum, ticket sales tripled.

Many felt this was Barnum's most shameless scam. Near the end of his life, he said he was "not proud" of the entire incident.[7] By the end of 1843, with the help of the dried-up old mermaid, Barnum had become the most famous showman in the United States and had earned the title "the prince of humbugs."[8]

Deception, hoaxing, humbugging, cheating—these were some of the words Americans commonly associated with Barnum during his lifetime and ever since. However, the appearance of morality was necessary to be a successful showman. Outright wickedness was not permitted while tempting the public to spend money on a regular basis. Barnum found his fortune when he took control of Scudder's American Museum. In the first three years of Barnum's management, the annual income of the museum increased steadily, growing to more than thirty thousand dollars per year.

"I must confess, " he wrote in his autobiography, "that I liked the Museum for the opportunities it afforded for rapidly making money."[9] Within a year, Barnum had repaid his debt to Olmsted. He now owned the museum outright. The American Museum would be Barnum's "ladder . . . to fortune."[10]

5

GENERAL TOM THUMB

Less than a year after his purchase of the American Museum, Barnum made a new discovery. In November 1842, while visiting his half brother Philo in Bridgeport, Connecticut, he was introduced to a "remarkably small child. . . . He was a . . . bright-eyed little fellow with light hair and ruddy cheeks. . . ."[1]

Four-year-old Charles Sherwood Stratton had stopped growing when he was seven months old. In fact, since his birth on January 4, 1838, the boy had gained fewer than six pounds. He stood twenty-five inches tall and weighed only fifteen pounds.

Charles's parents were poor. His father, Sherwood Stratton, was a carpenter. His mother, Cynthia, worked in a local inn. They were pleased when Barnum offered to hire Charles to appear as one of his curiosities for

My Dwarf

Barnum often referred to Charles Stratton as "my dwarf."[2] However, that term was inaccurate. A dwarf has a normal-sized upper body, but his or her legs are much too short. Charles, on the other hand, was a midget—a perfectly proportioned person on a smaller scale. His lack of growth was caused by a pituitary gland that did not produce enough hormones. The connection between the pituitary gland located at the base of the skull and growth problems was not discovered until 1886, three years after Charles Stratton's death.[3]

four weeks. The museum owner agreed to pay the boy four dollars a week. In addition, Sherwood Stratton would receive three dollars a week, plus room and board and travel expenses for Charles and his mother.

Again, Barnum used creative advertising to make his new exhibit popular. While he waited for his little curiosity to arrive in New York, the showman printed biographies of General Tom Thumb, the new name Barnum had selected for Charles. Thousands of lithographs, or engravings, were distributed. When Cynthia Stratton arrived, she was surprised to learn that her son had become "the rarest, the tiniest, the most diminutive dwarf imaginable—TOM THUMB, ELEVEN YEARS OLD AND ONLY TWENTY-FIVE INCHES HIGH, JUST ARRIVED FROM ENGLAND!!!"[4] To make his new attraction even more curious, Barnum had added seven years to Charles's age and had made him an English citizen.

Barnum named his new attraction after one of King Arthur's legendary knights. Legend claimed that Sir Tom Thumb dwelt in a tiny golden palace with a door one-inch wide. Six white mice pulled his coach. The tiny knight was mortally wounded during a duel with a spider.[5]

Barnum himself assumed the responsibility for Charles's training. He coached the boy for hours. Charles was eager to learn, had a talent for impersonation, and loved to show off on stage.[6] With the help of costumes, props, a few dance steps, and some songs, the four-year-old was transformed.

The auditorium was filled when General Tom Thumb made his debut in the American Museum lecture room on December 8, 1842. He opened with a monologue full of puns: "Good evening, ladies and gentlemen. I am only a Thumb, but a good hand in a general way at amusing you, for though a mite, I am mighty. . . ."[7]

During his act, Charles, or Tom Thumb, played several characters, including Cupid with a bow and quiver of arrows, a Revolutionary War soldier, David the giant slayer, and the role he is best remembered for—Napoleon Bonaparte, the former emperor of France. Tom Thumb also told the audience stories about himself and his life in England. Children were often invited on stage so that their heights might be compared with his. At the end of the month, Barnum

Barnum took responsibility for Charles Stratton's education, coaching him for hours in the roles he would play. The boy had a natural talent for mimicry, so he mastered the different characters quickly.

extended the boy's contract until January 1, 1844, and raised Tom's weekly pay to twenty-five dollars.

New Horizons

By January 1844, Barnum had accumulated some capital and decided to take Tom Thumb, his parents, and a tutor abroad. His intentions were to captivate Europe and make a name for himself on the other side of the Atlantic Ocean.

Before departing from the United States, Barnum arranged to send accounts of his experiences abroad to the *New York Atlas* newspaper. Besides providing readers with his impressions of Europe, these letters were part of his plan to keep the name of Barnum and the American Museum in the news.

Lost Childhood

The showman himself told stories of how Tom Thumb delighted in setting traps by running twine between chair and table legs and would "roll upon the floor and shed tears of joy" when his parents and Barnum pretended to trip over them.[8] However, in Barnum's haste to turn Charles into what the showman called "the man in miniature," the boy's natural development was all but forgotten.[9]

"I never had any childhood, any boy-life," Stratton complained later to his wife.[10] She recalled that her husband was particularly fond of children and liked to watch them play.

Barnum also made certain that no Tom Thumb revenues were lost. He exhibited the child until an hour before sailing. In fact, when the ship was delayed, posters were immediately printed announcing that "A few hours more remained for Tom Thumb to be seen at the American Museum."[11] When it was finally time to depart, a parade of ten thousand people led by a band escorted the little "general" to the docks. The group sailed for England on the *Yorkshire* on January 18, 1844. During the trip, Barnum focused on ways to promote Tom Thumb.

"Luck," the showman later wrote, "is in no sense the foundation of my fortune; from the beginning of my career I planned and worked for my success. To be sure," he admitted, "my schemes often amazed me with the affluence of their results, and . . . I sometimes 'builded [*sic*] better than I knew.'"[12]

Barnum's plan to excite British audiences was one of his most daring. The showman decided that Tom Thumb would "become the petted darling of the English . . . royal court."[13]

At the end of the eighteen-day voyage, Tom was smuggled past the crowds, posing as a babe in his mother's arms so no one would get a free peek. Barnum first exhibited General Tom Thumb for a few nights in Liverpool and London to announce his arrival. Then Barnum closed the show and settled into a furnished mansion in a fashionable part of London. Invitations to have tea with Tom were sent to a select number of noblemen and editors. The little general made a good impression on everyone.

Meanwhile, after securing American Ambassador Edward Everett's promise to arrange a meeting with Queen Victoria, Barnum rented a room in London's Egyptian Hall. At this site well-known for prestigious art shows and entertainments, the little general held daily exhibitions. Nothing short of the queen's "command" for Tom Thumb to appear at Buckingham Palace would stop the show.

Command Performance

On March 23, 1844, the twenty-five-year-old queen graciously received the tall showman and his tiny charge. Barnum later recorded many details of the historic meeting: The general, "looking like a wax-doll gifted with the power of locomotion," advanced with a firm step to the surprised queen and her circle at the far end of the royal picture gallery.[14]

Queen Victoria inquired about Tom Thumb's career. He amused her with his witty replies and asked for her son, the Prince of Wales, the future King Edward VII. She told him that the boy was asleep and that a meeting would be arranged in the near future. The visit lasted about an hour. Most of the time was devoted to the general's songs, dances, and imitations.

An amusing incident punctuated the end of the show. As Tom Thumb tried to follow instructions and back out of the long gallery, he was unable to keep up with Barnum. To compensate, the general would back up a few steps, then turn and run to catch up with Barnum, back up a few more steps and repeat the process. This so excited the queen's favorite poodle that it began barking and rushed after Tom Thumb. The general waved the tiny cane he had brought with him and engaged the dog in a "funny fight."[15] The amused queen immediately sent word that she hoped the general had "sustained no damage."[16]

Two more visits with the queen were arranged before another month passed. Barnum spent nearly one hundred pounds on an elegant court costume for Tom Thumb. Barnum also ordered a miniature carriage for the general. The coach, measuring only twenty inches high by eleven inches wide, was pulled by ponies only twenty-eight inches high. Children dressed in uniforms and wigs acted as coachmen. The outside of the carriage was painted blue and decorated with a coat of arms and the motto "Go Ahead." It had a silk-lined interior and windows of plate glass.

Royal patronage brought greater rewards than Barnum ever imagined. After the command performances, Tom Thumb became the rage of London. He was dubbed the "Pet of the Palace" by a local newspaper.[17] Children danced the General Tom Thumb Polka and played with Tom Thumb dolls and cutouts. English music halls rang with songs dedicated to him.

During the four months that Tom Thumb appeared at the Egyptian Hall, receipts averaged five hundred dollars a day. Barnum's expenses for himself and the Strattons were about one tenth of that amount. Even after Barnum signed a new contract that gave the Stratton family an equal share of the profits after expenses, the showman still averaged a profit of

In his miniature carriage, Tom Thumb took drives through a London park reserved for the British royal family.

eight hundred dollars a week and counted on clearing thirty-five thousand dollars that year.

During this successful stay in London, Barnum did report one real scare. While out for a drive in a full-sized carriage, his little moneymaker nearly suffered a fatal accident. Tom Thumb and his tutor, H. G. Sherman, decided to sit with the carriage driver to get a better view of the countryside. When the horse bolted and ran away with the carriage, they crashed into a high stone wall with such force that the horse broke its neck and the carriage was seriously damaged.

Barnum, who had been seated inside, jumped out and frantically began searching for Tom Thumb under the wreckage. But the child was nowhere to be seen. Then a tiny voice called from over the wall, "All right—There's no danger, don't be frightened."[18] It turned out that Sherman had taken the general in his arms, and at the last moment, had made a heroic leap over the wall into the soft field beyond.

Princely Gifts

Gifts given to Tom Thumb by members of the royal family became part of his exhibit. A miniature watch, complete with a chain, was made for the little general by order of the Queen Dowager Adelaide, whose deceased husband had been the previous king of England.

Paris, France

With Tom Thumb still drawing large crowds in Great Britain, Barnum turned over the day-to-day running of the company to Sherman and went to Paris, France, to attend a grand exposition of modern inventions and scientific discoveries. He hoped to buy automatons—gadgets that operated mechanically—and other objects to display in the American Museum.

While in Paris, Barnum could not resist playing the tourist. He strolled along the Champs-Elysees, a famous avenue in the heart of the city, saw the polka and the cancan performed, and climbed to the top of the Notre Dame, a famous cathedral that stands on an island in the River Seine. He inspected animals and horticultural exhibits and marveled at the treasures of Versailles, a royal palace southwest of Paris.

When he returned to England, Barnum set out on a whirlwind tour of the countryside. While in the town of Stratford-upon-Avon, the childhood home of the English playwright and poet William Shakespeare, he came up with an ambitious scheme—the purchase

*Barnum left Tom Thumb with his manager and toured the English
countryside around London.*

of Shakespeare's birthplace. The museum owner planned to dismantle the house, transport it to New York, and then reconstruct it for display at the American Museum. However, when his plans leaked out, several English gentlemen intervened and bought the birthplace for a Shakespeare Association. Barnum was forced to look elsewhere for new exhibits.

6

HUSBAND AND FATHER

After Barnum had been away from home for nearly nine months, he left Sherman to manage the Tom Thumb exhibition and returned to America. It was time to renew the lease on the American Museum's building and to make improvements. Barnum laid out a plan to add innovations, including the hat check, a place near the museum entrance where gentlemen could leave their hats. In return, each man received a check, or numbered card, that identified him as the hat's proper owner. Barnum picked up this idea while in London. He arranged to install gas lamps and new three-dimensional exhibits, called dioramas, depicting famous people in natural settings. He also wanted the lecture room, the museum's auditorium, expanded.

It took Barnum less than three weeks to make arrangements for all the improvements he wanted. By November 9, 1844, he was ready to sail back to England on the steamship *Great Western*. This time, he decided to take his wife and three daughters with him. Frances, their third child, had been born on April 11, 1844, while he was in Europe.

During the two weeks at sea, he entertained himself by playing jokes on his seasick wife and poking fun at her. Charity finally asked why he had invited her along. Barnum replied, "Now Charity, you know if I had [not] . . . you would have said it was because I did not want you."[1]

After the showman settled his family in a hotel in England, he rejoined his little general for a tour of Scotland and Ireland. Then in March 1845, Barnum, his family, and the troupe packed for France. Almost immediately, the showman and Tom Thumb were summoned to appear before King Louis Philippe at the Tuileries Palace in Paris. Three additional visits were made to the royal family and the king specifically asked to see Tom Thumb perform as Napoleon. Once again, Barnum had managed publicity royally. Parisians went crazy over the little general. The exhibition's income was bigger than ever.

When he was not managing Tom Thumb, Barnum took time to show Charity and his daughters Paris. They visited all the sights that had impressed him on his earlier visit, but Barnum soon discovered that Charity did not share his enthusiasm for Europe. Straitlaced and often sickly, Charity took a dim view

of most of the things her husband loved. She disliked both the theater and the opera. She was critical of Barnum's card playing, cigar smoking, and drinking.[2] By now, he was drinking heavily and did not mind admitting it.[3]

Pregnant for the fourth time, Charity wanted to go home to what she called "The happiest land in the world—the land of Sabbaths."[4] So in June 1845, Charity and the children sailed home.

Travel and Troubles

Barnum spent the next several months traveling in France, Belgium, and Spain before he made another trip home. When he arrived, he discovered that he had another daughter. Pauline had been born on March 1, 1846. Unfortunately, there was also sad news waiting. His daughter Frances had died shortly before her second birthday.

Barnum confided in a letter to a friend that something went wrong during this stay in America, "my troubles only seemed daily to increase."[5] It is likely that Charity, who had given birth to two of their children and seen the death of a third while Barnum was off on his rambles, was complaining about Barnum's decision to go back to Europe and stay for another year.

"In a fit of . . . *desperation*," the showman wrote, he set sail again.[6] Barnum remained overseas until the end of 1846. Then, after spending most of three years abroad, he headed home to take over his museum and to reacquaint himself with his wife and daughters.

*American artist Frederick Spencer painted this portrait of Barnum's
three daughters in 1847. Caroline would have been about fourteen,
Helen about six, and Pauline about one year old.*

Taking the Pledge

By this time, her husband's heavy drinking concerned Charity. Even Barnum began to fear that he might turn into a drunkard. After observing several prominent gentlemen staggering drunk at a Tom Thumb exhibition, the showman vowed never to touch whiskey again. However, he continued to consume a full bottle or more of champagne each evening. Soon, his drinking began to interfere with his ability to work full days.

This habit continued until Barnum attended a lecture given by his friend the Reverend Edwin Chapin on the subject of "The Moderate Drinker." The reverend claimed it was the moderate, or social, drinker whom young people looked to as an example that gave the whole habit of drinking a dangerous air of respectability. Chapin believed that the moderate

Family Vacation

On his return from Europe, Barnum took Charity and Caroline to see Niagara Falls. A flight of two hundred fifty steps led down to the ferry that took tourists across to the Canadian side of the falls. Charity had to be talked into attempting the descent. About halfway down she complained of dizziness and refused to go on. Barnum and his daughter left her there and continued on their way. When they returned to the American side later in the day, they learned that Charity had fainted on the stairs after they left and had been carried up by a party of men.

drinker's influence was the most evil of all. Much affected by this point of view, Barnum sat up all night thinking. Before dawn, he poured out the wine from all the bottles in his cellar. Then he went to Reverend Chapin and signed the teetotaler pledge—a solemn vow to stop drinking alcoholic beverages. From then on, Barnum passionately supported the temperance movement, which began around 1810 in the states of New York, Massachusetts, and Connecticut. The movement's main concern was the way drunkenness affected families. Temperance groups believed that alcohol should be restricted or even outlawed. They encouraged drinkers to stop entirely or to consume alcoholic beverages only in moderate quantities. By 1835, temperance organizations had about one million members nationwide. After taking the pledge, Barnum added his name to their membership and lectured everywhere on the evils of alcohol.

A New Man, a New Home

In the late 1840s, Barnum and Charity decided that Bridgeport, Connecticut, was the ideal location for their family home. The community was near enough to New York City, by rail and water, that Barnum could commute to his business. But it was far enough away to have the feeling of country living. Barnum purchased seventeen acres overlooking Long Island Sound, less than a mile east of Bridgeport, and began planning a home that suited a man of his wealth and success.

Barnum decided on the architecture for his mansion while touring England with Tom Thumb. His home was modeled after the ornate and gaudy Royal Pavilion located in Brighton, England. Work began during Barnum's final year abroad and his palace was to be constructed "regardless of cost."[7] Barnum employed five hundred local carpenters and laborers to complete the job quickly.

On November 14, 1848, the doors of the sandstone mansion were opened to more than one thousand guests. Barnum named his new home Iranistan. The finished house was three stories high. The mansion was topped with towers and a grand central dome that soared ninety feet.

The interior of the mansion was more stunning than the outside. Mirrored walls made large rooms seem even larger. Walls were covered with gilding, or very thin sheets of gold. Thick-piled carpet covered the floors. Paintings and statues decorated every wall and nook. A wide walnut staircase wound up to the conservatory in the central dome.

Barnum's private study was the most elegant of all. The walls and ceilings were hung with orange satin cloth, with furniture and rugs made to match.

Barnum installed the latest innovations in his new showplace. It was heated by hot air, equipped with burglar and fire alarms, and warmed by fuel from Barnum's own private gas works. Iranistan immediately became one of the sights to see in New England.

Barnum settled into a happy routine in his new home. He later wrote, "I count these two years—1848 and 1849—among the happiest of my life."[8] The showman followed a strict daily schedule. He got up at seven and spent the entire morning at his desk, answering letters and conducting business. Shortly after noon, he would go out for a carriage ride. When he returned to Iranistan, Barnum had a large midday meal, followed by a five-minute nap, which, he claimed, refreshed him as much as if he had slept for hours.

Evenings at Iranistan were carefully scheduled. Barnum liked to read for an hour, or listen to piano or string music. Most of all, he enjoyed having a few neighbors in for several games of whist and cribbage—popular card games of the time—or chess. However,

Iranistan was the most ornate home Barnum would ever live in.

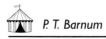

visitors were expected to leave by nine-thirty. If they forgot, Barnum bluntly told them that he intended to be in bed by ten.

Not quite forty, Barnum seemed to have accomplished everything he had expected of himself. He was rich. He was famous. He had a family and had built himself a palace fit for a king. But instead of thinking of retirement, the showman was about to launch his most ambitious scheme—one that would change his image from a humbug to a serious promoter of the arts.

7

RESPECT FOR A HUMBUG

In 1850, Barnum took his first steps toward a new image of respectability by promoting entertaining dramas that taught a moral lesson in the American Museum's newly renovated lecture room. The theater now seated three thousand in its main floor and two balconies. The museum owner focused on drawing women and families to his new theater. He claimed that "not a word" uttered on his stage would be "offensive to morals or religion"—not an easy task during the pre–Civil War decade.[1]

Abolitionists had convinced a growing number of Northerners that slavery was wrong and should not be allowed to spread to new territories in the West. In 1850, after months of debate over California's state-hood, the United States Congress passed a set of laws

that tried to satisfy both the North and South. These laws, known as the Compromise of 1850, banned slave trade—but not slavery itself—in Washington, D.C., and admitted California as a free state. They also made stricter laws to help slave owners catch and return runaway slaves.

One of Barnum's most popular stage productions in the late 1850s was Harriet Beecher Stowe's *Uncle Tom's Cabin*, a story that showed the cruelty of slavery. Barnum presented a version of Stowe's play written specifically for his lecture room. All the author's passionate attacks against slavery were removed so this production would not offend anyone. Even the story's tragic ending was transformed to a happy one.

With his usual flair for innovation, Barnum introduced matinees (afternoon showings) and continuous performances on holidays. His own permanent acting company performed a constantly changing variety of melodramas, comedies, and farces.

The Swedish Nightingale

Though Barnum's fame was growing, he still dreamed of changing his image to a serious promoter of the arts.[2] To accomplish this, he decided to sign Europe's most renowned classical singer, Jenny Lind, known as the Swedish Nightingale, to do a concert tour of America.

In January 1850, Barnum's agent, John Hall Wilton, signed a contract with Lind. The singer agreed to appear in one hundred fifty "concerts or oratorios" for one hundred fifty thousand dollars.[3] In addition, she

Though Jenny Lind was not strikingly beautiful, her charming singing voice held audiences spellbound across the country.

expected the expenses and salary for a maid, a valet, a secretary, and a friend. Barnum was to deposit the total amount in a bank before the group left Europe. The costs added up to $187,500—a figure equivalent to more than $1 million today.

Once the deal was made, Barnum realized he had a problem. Though Jenny Lind was the toast of Europe, only a handful of people in the United States knew her name. He had only eight months to educate the millions on whom he was depending to buy tickets.

Barnum immediately launched a publicity campaign to introduce Americans to Jenny Lind. Biographies were prepared and distributed. Her portrait was printed in newspapers, periodicals, and on handbills. Barnum hired an English journalist, who had once heard Lind sing, to write weekly news stories stressing her chastity, charity, and European triumphs.

By the time Lind's ship docked in New York Harbor in September 1850, "the wildest enthusiasm prevailed." Flags and triumphal arches awaited her on the wharf, Barnum remembered.[4] Lind's carriage could barely make its way through the crowds. Reporters estimated that there were thirty thousand people on hand to cheer her arrival.

Though Lind had not yet sung a single note, Barnum modified the original contract at once. He now offered Lind half the profits from each concert, after Barnum received fifty-five hundred dollars for his expenses and services. Requests and offers for Lind to perform came from all over the country. In a nine-month series of concerts, Jenny Lind traveled to

Boston; Providence; Philadelphia; New York; Baltimore; Washington, D.C.; Richmond; Charleston; Havana, Cuba; New Orleans; St. Louis; Cincinnati; and Louisville. The tour was a staggering success. However, when members of Jenny Lind's staff suggested that Barnum was keeping more of the profits than was fair,

Jenny Lind

Barnum arranged the tour without having heard Jenny Lind sing. He met the small, thirty-year-old brunette for the first time when her ship docked in New York Harbor. Lind had expressive blue eyes, broad cheekbones, and a wide mouth. Her face seemed almost plain, until she began to sing. Her biography, a rags to riches story, was perfect for Barnum's promotion.

Born in Stockholm, Sweden, in 1820, Jenny Lind moved from household to household with her bad-tempered, unmarried mother. Then one day, a dancer at the Royal Theater School heard the nine-year-old sing. Jenny Lind was the youngest student ever accepted by the Swedish Royal Theater School. Trained in acting, dancing, and voice, she sang with the Royal Theater and was appointed court singer by the king of Sweden. However, at age twenty, the intense singing and training began to affect her voice. Thankfully, after six weeks of doctor-prescribed rest, her voice recovered. The Swedish Nightingale, whose voice reminded many listeners of the warbling of a songbird, could sing again.

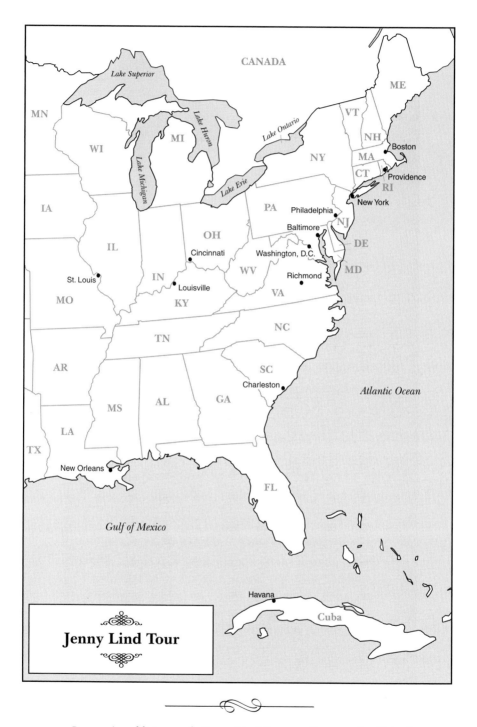

Jenny Lind Tour

Barnum's publicity made Jenny Lind famous all across the United States. Crowds flocked to hear the Swedish Nightingale in every city in which a concert was scheduled.

Lind grew distrustful of him. After her ninety-fifth concert, the singer broke her contract. Even then, Barnum collected $712,000 in less than a year.

The Jenny Lind tour is often regarded as one of Barnum's greatest feats. A close friend of Barnum's summed up its significance, saying: "Never, in the history of music or in the history of entertainment in America, has the advent of a foreign artist been hailed with so much enthusiasm . . . [and] a considerable portion of it was due to the shrewd and energetic advertising of Mr. Barnum."[5]

Writing, Real Estate, and Retirement

In the summer of 1854, Barnum retreated to Iranistan and began work on his memoirs. The 404-page book, entitled *The Life of P. T. Barnum, Written by Himself*, was published in mid-December. The refreshingly original work became an instant best-seller. One hundred sixty thousand copies sold the first year alone. *Knickerbocker Magazine* praised the volume as a true and reliable history, adding that Barnum's self-denial, frugality, industry, and temperance formed a model for his readers to emulate. Mark Twain, author of *Tom Sawyer* and *Huckleberry Finn*, is said to have sat up nights reading the book by lamplight.

In the summer of 1855, Barnum decided it was time to retire. He sold the American Museum collection of curiosities to his manager, John Greenwood, Jr. Then, he signed the lease for the museum building over to his wife.

Life Revised

Barnum's 1854 autobiography is one of the three or four best-known autobiographies in nineteenth-century America. As with everything Barnum promoted, his life story lived up to its promise. Biographer Neil Harris noted that it was "controversial and unexceptionable, candid and contrived, repetitious and arresting."[6] The work justified its author's life and achievements. In 1869, a revised autobiography, *Struggles and Triumphs*, was published.

Amazingly, the story of Barnum's life has not been out of print since it was first published in 1854. It has been printed again and again and caused a sensation on both sides of the Atlantic.

Charity, now forty-eight, was weak and often ill. She enjoyed little except puttering among her flowers in a greenhouse Barnum had built for her. His three daughters who "had been brought up," Barnum said with some regret, "in luxury; accustomed to call on servants to attend to every want," were their father's greatest pleasure.[7]

Caroline, a tall, slender, dark-eyed brunette, was Barnum's favorite. She had a first-rate business sense and a talent for conversation. She had married David Thompson in 1852. Helen, who had grown into a shapely brunette, is said to have resembled her father

Phineas Taylor Barnum, as portrayed in his first autobiography, published in 1854.

in looks and personality. Pauline, Barnum's youngest daughter, had a beautiful singing voice.

Misfortune

Several years before his retirement, Barnum had purchased fifty acres across the Pequonnock River from Bridgeport. Barnum and several partners intended to develop the area into a new city of East Bridgeport. In the early 1850s, they laid out tree-lined streets, began selling lots for homes, and discussed ways to attract businesses to the area.

In 1855, Barnum learned that the Jerome Clock Company might be persuaded to relocate. The company's president requested money to get the company through some hard times. In return for the loan, the clock company would move to East Bridgeport. After some consideration, Barnum agreed to lend the company fifty thousand dollars. He said he would accept responsibility for promissory notes, or written promises to pay a certain amount of money, for another sixty thousand. His total financial liability was to be limited to one hundred ten thousand dollars.

Unfortunately, the clock company used Barnum's notes again and again to satisfy creditors. By the time Barnum discovered what was happening, his liability was far beyond the limit. He was responsible for debts of more than half a million dollars.

When Barnum realized he was facing financial disaster, he quickly settled his personal debts. He did not want creditors who had trusted him to go unpaid.

In 1856, Barnum declared bankruptcy. He could scarcely believe what had happened.[8] Suddenly, he was poor. The family's only income was nineteen thousand dollars earned from the American Museum lease that was in Charity's name. Iranistan and all Barnum's personal property fell into the hands of creditors. Barnum moved his family into a rented house in New York City.

Though friends offered to help, Barnum declined, saying, "he must 'extricate' [free] himself from debt by his own efforts."[9] Legally, bankruptcy had limited his liability for the clock company debts, but Barnum was determined to pay off the notes completely and redeem his good name.

Among the many offers of assistance that he received, one touched and interested Barnum most of all. It arrived in the form of a note from eighteen-year-old Charles Stratton, who still performed on his own as General Tom Thumb: "My Dear Mr. Barnum, . . . I am ready to go on to New York, bag and baggage, and remain at . . . [your] service as long as I, in my small way, can be useful."[10]

At first, Barnum refused the young man. Less than a year later, however, Barnum accepted his offer, and together, they set off on a new European tour.

About a year after that, Barnum returned to America briefly to take care of some business and attend his daughter Helen's wedding to Samuel H. Hund. While he was home, another disaster struck. On the evening of December 17, 1857, Iranistan burned to the ground. Though the house was held by creditors, Barnum wrote, "My beautiful Iranistan was gone! This was not only a serious loss to my estate . . . but it was generally regarded as a public calamity. It was the only building in its peculiar style of architecture . . . in America."[11] Due to his circumstances, the house, which Barnum estimated to be worth one hundred fifty thousand dollars, was insured for only twenty-eight thousand dollars.

Sadly, Barnum rejoined Tom Thumb in Europe. At the suggestion of friends, he decided to try a new fund-raising idea—public lecturing. He prepared a lecture called *The Art of Money-Getting*, after telling friends that, "considering my clock complications, I thought I was more competent to speak on 'The Art of Money-Losing.'"[12] He made his debut as lecturer December 29, 1858, to enthusiastic reviews. The following year, he repeated his lecture almost one hundred times. An engaging, funny, often powerful speaker, Barnum drew large crowds wherever he went.

By 1860, with the help of Tom Thumb, his own lecturing, and a simple lifestyle, Barnum had repaid all his debts. Financially independent once again, he repurchased the American Museum collection and prepared for a new chapter in his life.

8

REBUILDING DREAMS

For nearly five years, the Barnums had lived in rented houses and apartments. Now that all his debts were repaid, Barnum decided it was time to build again. The family's new home, Lindencroft, was located about one thousand feet from the old site of Iranistan. Once construction was under way, Barnum turned his attention to the American Museum. It was also in need of rebuilding. During the last five years, the owners had not updated or added to the exhibits, and the museum's popularity had declined.

Barnum immediately enlarged and modernized the building, expanded his curiosities, rearranged displays, and created a special 112-page illustrated guidebook

to direct families through the museum's Seven Grand Saloons, or exhibit rooms. After purchasing a twenty-five-cent ticket, a visitor entered a ground floor that was filled with 194 original dioramas—scenes of Italy, Egypt, Russia, and other exotic countries around the world.

The second floor contained a variety of exhibits including a fortune-teller, giantesses, dwarfs, portraits of famous men, and also Barnum's private office. The third floor contained case after case of curiosities. For example, the contents of case number 794 were: "Ball of Hair found in the stomach of a sow; Indian collar, composed of grizzly bear claws; the sword of a sword fish . . . ; African pocket-book; Chinese pillow; a petrified piece of pork . . . ; fragment of the first canal-boat which reached New York City . . . , " and much more.[1]

Tropical plants, tanks for reptiles, and Ned the Learned Seal, who played musical instruments, could be seen on the fourth floor. The fifth floor was the home of Barnum's "Happy Family"—monkeys, dogs, mice, cats, pigeons, owls, porcupines, guinea pigs, roosters, and even boa constrictors. This odd collection of predator and prey animals had been trained to get along together. Cats and mice, for example, played together in one exhibit. Other animal exhibits, such as pigeons painted colors no naturalist had ever found, and a boa constrictor in the act of striking, made visitors wonder if they could believe all they saw.

The sixth floor displayed minerals and insects. The top floor, under open skylights, was alive with wild animals Barnum had collected from around the world. Even the basement contained tanks of fish and more animals.

Under Barnum's management, the American Museum again became a tourist attraction not to be missed, even by royalty. In 1860, the Prince of Wales, the future King Edward VII, became the first member of the British royal family to visit the United States. Barnum's museum was "[t]he only place of amusement in America honored" by his presence.[2] Barnum quickly noted this triumph in his guidebook. The museum owner, however, was not on hand for the royal visit, and the prince stated that he was sorry to have missed "the most extraordinary curiosity in the establishment"—Barnum himself.[3]

Civil War

As Barnum rebuilt his business, he was constantly alert to the changing political climate. The country was on the brink of civil war, as the states of the North and the South divided over the issues of slavery and states' rights. Barnum, who was opposed to slavery, supported the Republican presidential candidate, Abraham Lincoln, who wanted to prevent the spread of slavery to the West. Lincoln's election as the country's sixteenth president caused several Southern states to secede, or withdraw, from the Union and form a new nation—the Confederate States of America. Then, on April 12, 1861, Confederate troops fired on Fort Sumter in Charleston, South Carolina. The Civil War had begun.

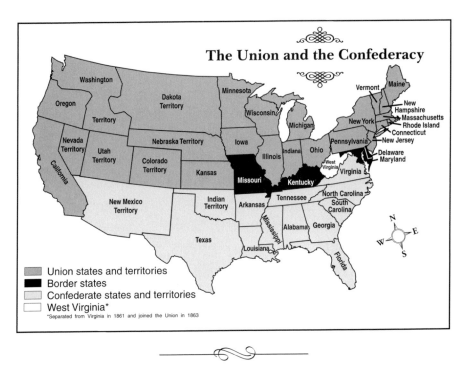

When the Civil War divided the United States, Barnum spoke out strongly in support of the Union cause. It was feared that his property would be targeted by Confederate sympathizers.

At fifty-one, Barnum was too old to enlist in the army. Instead, as was the custom among the rich, he paid for four substitute soldiers to represent him and contributed generously to the Union cause.[4] Barnum also joined the Prudential Committee, a group organized to prevent sabotage and treason.

Not everyone in his home state supported the Union cause. Many Connecticut residents sympathized with the South and wanted peace at any cost. When Barnum learned that such a group was holding a rally about ten miles north of Bridgeport, he attended the meeting in the company of several Union soldiers who were home on leave. When the orator began to speak of Northern aggression, the soldiers charged the platform and chased him off. Then Barnum was carried to the platform, where he made a speech full of patriotism and spiced with humor.

One of the lesser-known sidelights of the Civil War was a Confederate plot to burn New York City. Barnum's American Museum became one of the targets.[5] Eight Confederate officers planned to set fires all over New York City. After setting three fires, one of the Confederates, Captain Robert C. Kennedy, got caught in the crowd in front of Barnum's American Museum. Afraid he would be recognized, Kennedy paid admission to the museum and ducked inside for safety. Then, the Confederate soldier realized he was in the perfect spot for a spectacular fire. He opened his valise and hurled a bomb down the main staircase. There was a sudden sheet of flames and the museum was on fire. Fortunately, the people and animals escaped unharmed. When the fire was out, Barnum estimated that only about a thousand dollars' worth of damage had been done. Other fires set around the city were also put out quickly and the Confederate plot failed. All the Southern officers involved escaped to Toronto, Canada, by train.

During the war years, record numbers flocked to Barnum's American Museum. Patriotic dramas were presented twice daily in the lecture room. Popular programs included a twelve-year-old drummer boy, Robert Hendershot, who had survived the Battle of

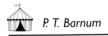
Fredericksburg, and an actress turned Northern spy, Pauline Cushman. She described her duties and adventures for the crowds, then did a series of quick changes to show the power of military disguise.

Wartime Wedding

To foster patriotic spirit, Tom Thumb was joined by two new, very American midgets. Barnum named them General Grant, Jr., and Commodore George Washington Morrison Nutt.

However, when both Nutt and Thumb fell in love with Lavinia Bump, another midget employed by Barnum, a miniature war erupted under the museum roof. Thumb won the skirmish, and on February 10, 1863, twenty-five-year-old Tom Thumb and twenty-one-year-old Mercy Lavinia Warren Bump were married at Grace Church in New York City. After the ceremony, the petite couple stood on top of a grand piano to greet the two thousand guests who attended their reception at the Metropolitan Hotel. Barnum paid for the wedding, and the publicity increased museum ticket sales. The bride and groom took a honeymoon tour of Philadelphia, Baltimore, and Washington, D.C., where they were President Lincoln's guests of honor at a White House reception.

A New Era

In 1865, Barnum was elected as Fairfield's representative to the Connecticut state legislature. As a Republican legislator, the showman voted for the abolition of slavery. He also made an impassioned

Tom Thumb's marriage to Lavinia Warren Bump revitalized his career. Advertisements like this one captured the public's interest in the tiny couple. The year after the wedding, the couple left for a successful three-year tour of Europe.

speech supporting an amendment to the Connecticut Constitution that eliminated the word *white* from the qualifications to vote. Despite his efforts, the amendment did not pass.

Barnum was in Hartford, Connecticut, addressing the state legislature when he received the news by

The War Ends

The country went into a week of celebration at the news of Confederate General Robert E. Lee's surrender at Appomattox Court House, Virginia, on April 9, 1865. The Civil War ended shortly afterward, and the Union was preserved. But only days later, the nation mourned President Abraham Lincoln's assassination by John Wilkes Booth. These significant events of celebration and mourning went unnoted in Barnum's autobiography.

telegram that disaster had struck his American Museum. Shortly after noon on July 13, 1865, a fire started in the museum's boiler room and spread through the building. The birds were set free at the first alarm. The whale tank was broken in hopes of dousing the flames. Ned the seal was saved by a fireman. When other animals, including snakes and a tiger, escaped and ran through the street, they caused panic among the thousands of spectators watching the fire. Some people were injured, but no one was killed.

Many of Barnum's human curiosities had to be rescued from the upper floors of the museum. Anna Swan, the Nova Scotia Giantess, who stood seven feet eleven inches tall, made the most dramatic escape. Firemen first had to chop a huge opening in the building wall before eighteen firemen worked together to lower the large woman safely to the ground.

Almost nothing was saved except the day's receipts. Barnum wrote that, when the fire was out, he had lost "an assemblage of rarities which a half million . . . dollars could not restore, and a quarter of a century could not collect."[6] He estimated the total loss of his collection to be about four hundred thousand dollars, and Barnum was insured for only forty thousand.

Barnum's first instinct was to quit. However, these comments published in a *New York Tribune* editorial inspired the museum owner to give it another try:

Fire plagued Barnum throughout his career. His American Museum burned twice. And in 1885, the main building at his circus winter quarters in Bridgeport also burned. In each case, many of the animals were killed. Though distressed by the tragic losses, Barnum quickly purchased more animals for his exhibits.

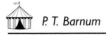
Barnum's Museum is gone, but Barnum himself, happily, did not share the fate of his rattlesnakes. . . . There are fishes in the seas and beasts in the forest; birds still fly in the air, and strange creatures still roam in the deserts; giants and pigmies still wander up and down the earth; the oldest man, the fattest woman, and the smallest baby are still living, and Barnum will find them.[7]

Incredibly, in September 1865, on the site of the old museum, Barnum's New American Museum opened its doors. Barnum had been busy during the six weeks since the fire. Advertisements claimed that, by

Political Defeat

In February 1867, following two successful terms in the Connecticut legislature, Barnum was nominated as the Republican candidate from Connecticut for the United States Congress. He accepted the nomination and began a spirited campaign against the Democratic candidate. But old prejudices against showmen resurfaced.

On March 5, 1867, the *New York Evening Express* published a piece entitled "Barnum's First Speech in Congress." It claimed to be a "prediction 'by spiritual telegraph' of what floods of rhetoric might be expected if indeed he was successful in the election."[8] The article, written by Mark Twain, ridiculed the idea of Barnum as a serious candidate. Barnum was defeated after an ugly campaign and gave up politics in disgust.

opening day, one hundred thousand new curiosities had already been collected for the public to view.

Unfortunately, less than three years later, on March 3, 1868, the New American Museum burned to the ground. Fire again destroyed Barnum's collection and the hundreds of animals inside. It happened on one of the coldest nights of the year. Snow-filled streets delayed the horse-drawn fire wagons, and "the water froze almost as soon as it left the hose of the fire engines," the museum owner remembered.[9] Barnum accepted this fire as notice to get out of the museum business.

Barnum's eighty-three-year-old mother, Irena, died in 1868. His wife's health was also growing steadily worse. In 1869, Barnum sold Lindencroft and moved into an elaborate summer manor on Long Island Sound called Waldemere, which means wood near the sea. For the next few years, Barnum lived a quiet life out of the spotlight.

9

UNDER THE
BIG TOP

Afterfire destroyed his American Museum for a
second time, Barnum decided to quit the business, saying, "I have done work enough, and shall play
the rest of my life."[1] At first, the showman enjoyed his
retirement, but after a few months of reading, "writing without any special purpose," playing parlor
games, attending lectures, concerts, operas, and dinner parties, Barnum wrote that he felt "like the truant
schoolboy . . . [who] had no play-mate."[2]

For forty years, he had led an active business life.
At fifty-eight, Barnum was still a healthy man. He was
not content to spend quiet evenings at home with his
invalid wife. So when Charity was well enough to be
left alone, he began to arrange tours for more curiosities and to travel with an English friend, John Fish,

whom he had met while lecturing on *The Art of Money-Getting.*

Together, Barnum and Fish toured Niagara Falls and the island of Cuba, then steamed up the Mississippi River after sightseeing in New Orleans. They traveled west by train to Salt Lake City, Utah, where Barnum met Brigham Young, the leader of the Mormon Church. During these travels, Fish shared letters from his twenty-year-old daughter, Nancy, with Barnum. Attracted by the young woman's lively prose, Barnum began to correspond with her.

From Utah, the two men traveled on to San Francisco, California. There, Barnum purchased sea lions to show in New York and discovered a midget smaller then Tom Thumb, hired him, and named him Admiral Dot. Their trip continued to Yosemite Valley, which Barnum found "wonderful, wonderful, sublime, indescribable, incomprehensible; I never saw anything so truly and appallingly grand. . . ."[3]

However, after a couple of years, travel lost its excitement. By the fall of 1870, Barnum was ready for a change.[4] When William Cameron Coup, a young circus manager, and Don Costello, Coup's partner, asked Barnum to help start up a circus, he agreed.

The Circus

Barnum did not invent the circus. It had existed since the days of ancient Egypt and Rome. The first circuses to tour America were small troupes of performers and clowns. In 1820, menageries were added to emphasize the show's educational value. A small circus could be loaded into two wagons. A larger show might need forty horses, eight wagons, and have thirty-five performers.

In April 1871, P. T. Barnum's Grand Traveling Museum, Menagerie, Caravan, and Circus opened in Brooklyn beneath three acres of canvas tent—an immense improvement on early American shows.

By flickering gaslights, ten thousand spectators watched the largest circus ever attempted in the United States. There were sixty stars and performers, seventy-five full-time employees, and one hundred wagons. An amazing success, Barnum's traveling circus made four hundred thousand dollars during its first year touring the eastern and midwestern United States.

By 1872, more than twenty-six thousand miles of railroad track crisscrossed the country, and Barnum's circus began traveling by train. Though smaller shows were already using trains, until this time, large shows had been limited by the distances horses could pull wagons overnight. Barnum's circus was the first of its size to travel by rail. His partner, Coup, figured out all the details to pack and move the show. The tents would come down after the final evening performance, and by night, the circus would be loaded on train cars and moved to its next location. On the following morning, five acres of Big Top, enough to cover a museum, menagerie, hippodrome (or oval track for chariot racing), and a two-ring show, would spring magically to life—or so it seemed—in a new town.

Because the success of this huge operation depended on getting the people to the show, Coup

Experience, Experience, Experience

Barnum always considered himself primarily a promoter and museum man. In fact, he did not become a full-time circus owner until after his sixtieth birthday. However, his prior experience prepared Barnum for his last and best remembered career.

In 1836, he had traveled with Aaron Turner, one of the pioneers of the American circus. Twelve years later, Barnum and partner Seth B. Howes, another experienced showman, organized and promoted the Great Asiatic Caravan, Museum, and Menagerie, as much a traveling version of Barnum's American Museum as a circus. These experiences, along with the knowledge he had gained by running the museum, taught Barnum all he needed to know about the three elements that made up 1870s circus performances:

- The menagerie, where wild and unusual animals were displayed
- The sideshow, where "freaks" or living oddities could be viewed
- The variety show, featuring clowns, jugglers, high-wire acts, trapeze artists, bareback riders, and trained dogs

also persuaded the railroads to run excursion trains at reduced rates for circus customers. This strategy allowed the circus to bypass smaller towns and still reach larger audiences. This new way to reach audiences set off a frenzy of change in the circus business—changes designed to draw more of the country's growing population to the Big Top.

By this time in Barnum's life, everything had to be the biggest, the grandest, the most spectacular.[5] In 1872, the main tent seated twelve thousand spectators. A second ring was added. Now audiences could watch two performances simultaneously. The circus, called P. T. Barnum's Great Traveling Exposition and World's Fair, made record-breaking profits.

In August 1872, Barnum decided to open an indoor circus that would employ two hundred circus entertainers during the winter. He purchased the Hippotheatron buildings on Fourteenth Street in New York, and his new show opened in November. Unfortunately, just before Christmas, the buildings burned to the ground. Barnum lost giraffes, polar bears, tigers, lions, sea lions, camels, pelicans, apes, and gorillas, along with costumes and equipment.

He immediately ordered more costumes and equipment and organized Barnum's Traveling World's Fair. Before the show's grand opening, all the costumed performers and wild animals paraded through the streets of New York, thrilling the thousands who gathered to watch. Unfortunately, this exciting tradition is no longer part of a modern circus performance. In some communities, when the circus arrives in town, the elephants do walk from the train station to the circus arena. As enormous as these creatures are, they still cannot compare with the gilded wagons, costumed riders, silly clowns, and the rolling menagerie that made Barnum's circus parades so magical.

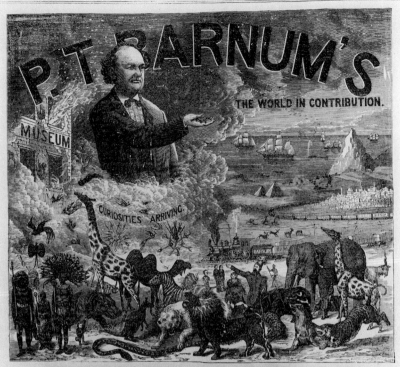

Barnum's advertisement for his Great Traveling World's Fair in Harper's Weekly, *on March 29, 1873.*

Wives

During Barnum's first years with the circus, Charity Barnum's illness was diagnosed as valvular heart disease, and her health continued to fail. Barnum was abroad in Europe purchasing wild animals for the circus when he received a telegram letting him know that his mate of forty-four years had died from a stroke on November 20, 1873. Her obituary noted that Charity Barnum was a woman of superior natural gifts and had been the valued and endeared companion of her husband.

It was impossible for Barnum to attend the funeral, but he spent several weeks in London in seclusion. While there, he was comforted by his old friend John Fish and Fish's daughter Nancy. Just thirteen weeks later, on February 14, 1874, Barnum and Nancy Fish were secretly married. Not a hint of this wedding has ever been found in family records. The marriage certificate was discovered one hundred twenty years later in the records of Middlesex County, England.[6]

Surrounded by family and friends, the couple was married again in New York City on September 16, 1874, ten months after Charity's death. The new Mrs. Barnum moved into Waldemere, the home Barnum had last shared with Charity. At age twenty-four, Nancy was younger than her three married stepdaughters. Barnum was sixty-four.

Barnum's daughters were not exactly pleased with their father's new bride. According to a story passed down through the family, when Barnum and Nancy arrived home after their honeymoon, the family greeted them on Waldemere's porch dressed in their best mourning clothes.

Circus Days

For a long time, Barnum had dreamed of a permanent circus in New York City. In 1873, he built an indoor coliseum, enormous for the time. The brick and cement building was 425 feet long and 28 feet high with an oval arena in the center. The structure provided seating for ten thousand beneath a partially enclosed roof. In bad weather the open-air arena could be tented over with canvas.

Barnum's Great Roman Hippodrome opened in April 1874. For two years, the show played in its new home in New York City and also traveled throughout New England, the Midwest, and to Ontario, Canada. The road version included a live English hunt with one hundred fifty riders, daily balloon flights by Professor W. H. Donaldson, chariot races involving strong, powerful women called Amazons,

Barnum's second wife, Nancy Fish Barnum, was younger than her three married stepdaughters.

and real cowboys, American Indians, and buffalo of the West. Around sixty-five railroad cars were needed to feed, sleep, and transport the twelve hundred circus employees and all the live animals.

Barnum focused all his energy on promoting his Great Roman Hippodrome with a twenty-four-page illustrated newspaper, *P. T. Barnum's Advance Courier*. It proved to be one of his most effective and widely copied ideas. The newspaper was first used by Barnum to promote his 1871 circus. It was distributed free in every town a week before the circus arrived. Written almost entirely by Barnum, the *Courier* was largely responsible for making the Roman Hippodrome

Nancy Barnum
The years Barnum shared with Nancy were happy ones. Barnum sometimes referred to his bride as his "little wife." Nancy's relationship with her husband's family eventually became friendly. She was always just Nancy to his children and Aunt Nancy to his grandchildren. Barnum was proud of his young English bride.

Nancy Barnum was an intelligent woman, a gifted pianist, and a published writer. At age forty, Nancy wrote a magazine article offering advice to other wives: "Share his pleasures. Take your holidays together. . . . Don't spend your summer in the mountains and at the seashore, leaving him in the city; and don't stay at home in the autumn while he goes to Europe. . . ."[7]

Circus one of the most successful shows of Barnum's career.

By now, Barnum and his partners had a million-dollar business with plans to open as many as a dozen different exhibitions in the United States and Europe. But all was not well. There was disagreement between them, though the issue is unclear. Coup and Costello may have objected to a sideline venture of Barnum's. The showman was making additional money by renting his face, name, and even his ads to competing shows. Or it may have been Barnum's refusal to consider cutting costs after the income from the circus declined for a season. Whatever the cause of the trouble, Coup and Costello finally resigned from the partnership in 1875.

Mayor of Bridgeport

That same year, Barnum formed another partnership with John Nathans, George Bailey, Avery Smith, and Lewis June, who were all experienced in the circus and menagerie business. Then, Barnum once again turned his attention to politics.

In 1875, some Republican friends asked Barnum to run for mayor of Bridgeport, Connecticut. However, the circus owner remembered all too well the criticism he received during his campaign for a seat in the United States Congress. He did not agree to run until prominent Democrats assured him that they, too, would support him. Barnum ran with his usual amount of energy, and was elected to a one-year term in 1875.

As mayor, Barnum worked for a better water and drainage system and for public baths, places where anyone could take a bath since most homes did not have running water or bathtubs. He commissioned new gas lighting for Bridgeport's streets and supported the efforts of African Americans to become members of local trade unions. Because of his stand on temperance, he strictly enforced liquor licenses and Sunday saloon closures. He also worked for lower utility rates.

Best of Barnum

In the fall of 1875, Mayor Barnum was approached by James Redpath's Lyceum Bureau, the finest speaker's bureau in the country. It boasted among its clients such giants as Ralph Waldo Emerson, Mark Twain, and Harriet Beecher Stowe. Redpath asked Barnum to deliver a series of twenty lectures in towns across New England.

These programs showed the best of Barnum. His talks were always light-spirited and fun, peppered throughout with original phrases of his own creation. He liked honest, down-to-earth English. Instead of labeling an object inexpensive, Barnum said it was dog-cheap. A giant woman was a whopper. Barnum also liberally used expressions such as "I am happy as a clam in high water."[8] Crowds everywhere chuckled at his unique brand of humor, funny stories, and even the occasional magic trick thrown in for good measure.

Though Barnum devoted all his energy to his job, by the end of the term, he discovered that one year was just not enough time to make major changes. Tired of fighting with other council members who did not see a need for reform, Barnum presided over his last common council meeting on March 29, 1876. Local newspapers praised his administration, but the showman went back to his amusements.

By the end of his mayoral term, Barnum was already planning an even bigger, better, grander circus project. Using a winning formula he would never again depart from, the circus promoter organized one enormous circus, with separate tents for the museum and menagerie, and a Big Top that contained a hippodrome track and circus rings. The title, P. T. Barnum's Greatest Show on Earth, had first been used in 1872, when Barnum, Coup, and Costello were partners. However, Barnum's newest project would live up to that name and would be remembered as the Greatest Show on Earth.

10

THE GREATEST SHOW ON EARTH

Throughout the late 1870s, no other circus could match the amazing and varied entertainment staged under Barnum's Big Top. Then, in 1880, the owners of the Great London Circus decided to challenge the showman for a share of the audiences in the eastern and midwestern United States.

Barnum was aware of his competition and watched with envy as an elephant brought overnight fame to the Great London Circus by giving birth to the first elephant born in America. Barnum wanted the baby, Little Columbia, and the publicity for himself. When he offered one hundred thousand dollars for her, the owners wired back: "Will not sell at any price."[1] Instead, they pulled a publicity stunt worthy of the showman himself and published enlarged copies of Barnum's check in their circus flyers and handbills.

Impressed with the younger men whose business talents and energy matched his own, seventy-year-old Barnum signed a partnership with the owners of the Great London Circus, James A. Bailey and James E. Cooper, on August 26, 1880.[2] Eventually, Cooper sold his share, leaving Barnum and Bailey to form the successful partnership that would create the Greatest Show on Earth.

The Barnum and London Circus opened in New York City on March 1881 in Madison Square Garden, the former site of Barnum's Hippodrome. For the first time, acts were performed simultaneously in three circus rings. "The only drawback," the *New York Herald*

In 1873, the Greatest Show on Earth consisted of several tents through which spectators walked on their way to the Big Top to see the main attractions.

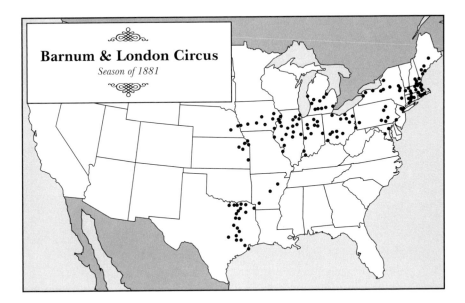

Barnum & London Circus
Season of 1881

	APRIL	MAY	JUNE	JULY	AUGUST	SEPTEMBER	OCTOBER	NOVEMBER
1	New York, NY	SUNDAY	Lowell, MA	Saratoga Springs, NY	Indianapolis, IN	Chicago, IL	Marshaltown, IA*	Marlis, TX
2	New York, NY	Scranton, PA	Lawrence, MA	Utica, NY	Crawfordsville, IN	Chicago, IL	SUNDAY	Calvert, TX
3	New York, NY	Wilkes-Barre, PA	Salem, MA	SUNDAY	Lafayette, IN	Chicago, IL	Oskaloosa, IA	Corsicana, TX
4	New York, NY	Reading, PA	Lynn, MA	Watertown, NY	Legansport, IN	SUNDAY	Des Moines, IA	Wasahachie, TX
5	New York, NY	Newark, NJ	SUNDAY	Syracuse, NY	Peru, IN	Aurora, IL	Atlantic, IA	McKinney, TX
6	New York, NY	Paterson, NJ	Boston, MA	Auburn, NY	Ft. Wayne, IN	Ottawa, IL	Council Bluffs, IA	SUNDAY
7	New York, NY	Jersey City, NJ	Boston, MA	Rochester, NY	SUNDAY	Joliet, IL	Omaha, NB	Bonham, TX
8	New York, NY	SUNDAY	Boston, MA	Lockport, NY	Toledo, OH	Bloomington, IL	Lincoln, NB	Paris, TX
9	New York, NY	Brooklyn, NY	Boston, MA	Buffalo, NY	Norwalk, OH	Springfield, IL*	SUNDAY	Texarkana, TX
10	New York, NY	Brooklyn, NY	Boston, MA	SUNDAY	Cleveland, OH	Decatur, IL	St. Joseph, MO	Hope, AR
11	New York, NY	Brooklyn, NY	Boston, MA	Detroit, MI	Youngstown, OH	SUNDAY	Atchison, KS	Little Rock, AR
12	New York, NY	Brooklyn, NY	SUNDAY	Ann Arbor, MI	Akron, OH	Peoria, IL	Topeka, KS	Newport, AR
13	New York, NY	Brooklyn, NY	Bangor, ME	Lansing, MI	Canton, OH	Oglesburg, IL	Lawrence, KS	END OF SEASON
14	New York, NY	Brooklyn, NY	Augusta, ME	Bay City, MI	SUNDAY	Burlington, IA	Kansas City, MO	
15	New York, NY	SUNDAY	Bath, ME	E. Saginaw, MI	Pittsburgh, PA	Quincy, IL	Ft. Scott, KS	
16	New York, NY	Bridgeport, CT	Lewiston, ME	Jackson, MI	Pittsburgh, PA	Jacksonville, IL	SUNDAY	
17	SUNDAY	Waterbury, CT	Portland, ME	SUNDAY	Wheeling, WV	Jerseyville, IL	Gainesville, TX	
18	Washington, D.C.	New Haven, CT	Dover, NH	Grand Rapids, MI	Zanesville, OH	SUNDAY	Greenville, TX	
19	Washington, D.C.	Meriden, CT	SUNDAY	Muskegon, MI	Columbus, OH	St. Louis, MO	Mineola, TX	
20	Baltimore, MD	Hartford, CT	Haverhill, MA	Allegan, MI	Chillicothe, OH	St. Louis, MO	Danison, TX	
21	Baltimore, MD	Holyoke, MA	Manchester, NH	Kalamazoo, MI	SUNDAY	St. Louis, MO	Sherman, TX	
22	Harrisburg, PA	SUNDAY	Concord, NH	Battle Creek, MI	Cincinnati, OH	St. Louis, MO	Dallas, TX	
23	Lancaster, PA	Springfield, MA	Nashua, NH	South Bend, IN	Cincinnati, OH	St. Louis, MO	SUNDAY	
24	SUNDAY	Norwich, CT	Fitchburg, MA	SUNDAY	Cincinnati, OH	St. Louis, MO	Galveston, TX	
25	Philadelphia, PA	Worcester, MA	Greenfield, MA	Kankakee, IL	Dayton, OH	SUNDAY	Houston, TX	
26	Philadelphia, PA	Woonsocket, RI	SUNDAY	Champaign, IL	Springfield, OH	Davenport, IA	Navasota, TX	
27	Philadelphia, PA	Providence, RI	Pittsfield, MA	Danville, IL	Richmond, IN	Iowa City, IA	Bryan, TX	
28	Philadelphia, PA	Fall River, MA	Albany, NY	Terre Haute, IN	SUNDAY	Rock Island, IL	Brenham, TX	
29	Philadelphia, PA	SUNDAY	Poughkeepsie, NY	Vincennes, IN	Chicago, IL	Clinton, IA	Austin, TX*	
30	Philadelphia, PA	New Bedford, MA	Troy, NY	Evansville, IN	Chicago, IL	Cedar Rapids, IA	SUNDAY	
31		Brockton, MA		SUNDAY	Chicago, IL		Waco, TX	

March 28–31—New York

* canceled

During the 1881 season, Barnum and Bailey's Greatest Show on Earth performed in towns from New York to Texas.

commented, was that, while the spectator's "head was turned in one direction, he felt that he was losing something good in another."[3]

Throughout the 1880s, Barnum attempted to outdo himself, again and again, with specialty acts. In 1882, Barnum topped even his own expectations with the purchase of Jumbo from the London Zoo. The outrage of British citizens, fueled at first by the English newspapers, then by the elephant's sit-down strike, caused a sensation in the United States, and Jumbo-mania swept the country.

"[The elephant] was the greatest free advertising . . . " Barnum once told a friend. "It never cost me a cent to advertise Jumbo."[4] He recognized the public's infatuation with his huge star and encouraged Matthew Scott, Jumbo's trainer, to write the elephant's biography. Barnum even arranged for Jumbo to test the strength of New York's Brooklyn Bridge. Crowds lined both sides of the river to watch the huge beast plod across the bridge from Manhattan to Brooklyn. The bridge stood the test, although Scott was afraid that the elephant would begin to dance to the loud vibrations caused by its own footsteps.

Cruel Accusations

Not everyone was captivated by Barnum and his three-ring circus. Charges of cruelty to animals and to children were filed several times against the circus owner. When Barnum hired the Elliotts, a family of child bicyclists, ages six through sixteen, Elbridge T. Gerry, president of the Society for the Prevention of

Cruelty to Children, filed charges. He claimed that the children were exhausted and that performing was endangering their health and safety. To disprove the charges, Barnum arranged a special exhibition of the fast-pedaling bike act for leading members of New York's medical and legal professions. The three judges who heard the case were part of that audience. When physicians declared the children's exercises to be "very beautiful and beneficial to their health," the court found Barnum not guilty.[5] Once again the free publicity helped promote Barnum's circus.

Complaints were also filed by Henry Bergh, founder of the American Society for the Prevention of Cruelty to Animals (ASPCA). He considered Barnum "a semi-barbarian" for keeping museum animals in cramped, dark, unventilated quarters, and for feeding snakes live prey.[6]

The society had every right to be concerned about circus animals. It was common practice in Africa and elsewhere to kill the parents so the young could be captured more easily, to cut elephants' tendons to bring them to their knees, and to transport wildlife by camelback for long distances in close, confining boxes. However, there was little public support for these concerns. At that time, most people believed that God put animals on the planet to serve mankind, and Bergh's protests were free publicity for Barnum. However, people feel much differently today. Circus owners expect protesters in every city where the circus performs. The animal rights movement is now a major threat to the circus industry.

As the circus used more animals, Bergh's inspections increased. Bergh's final battle with Barnum was over Salamander, a horse trained to leap through fiery hoops. When Bergh protested, Barnum challenged him to witness the act. Instead, Bergh sent an assistant named Hatfield, seven aides, and twenty policemen. While thousands watched, Salamander was led into the ring and the hoops were lit. Then Barnum, followed by ten clowns and Salamander, walked through one of the burning rings. The showman invited Bergh's assistant to step through the ring. Hatfield emerged unsinged. Five years later, Barnum joined the ASPCA and became one of Bergh's close friends.

To London

In 1889, Barnum did something he had been thinking about for almost ten years. He took his circus to London for a one-hundred-day engagement. Though not certain of his own reception in England after "stealing" Jumbo away, Barnum and Bailey felt certain their show would draw large crowds, since European circuses had only one ring and were tiny by comparison.

The menagerie, bandwagons, herds of horses, Roman chariots, tons of posters, and more than twelve hundred employees were loaded aboard an ocean liner to cross the Atlantic. Bailey organized the transportation magnificently. Seventy-nine-year-old Barnum, accompanied by his wife, Nancy, traveled with the show to handle publicity.

The Greatest Show on Earth opened to rave reviews as crowds of twelve thousand packed performances

Keeping up With the Times

Technology modernized America between 1840 and 1880. A transatlantic telegraph line was completed between the United States and Europe in 1850. The transcontinental railroad made it possible to travel across the United States in one week by 1869.

In 1876, Alexander Graham Bell, an American inventor, made the first call with his invention, the telephone. Thomas Alva Edison built the phonograph in 1877, then lit up the world in 1879 with the electric lightbulb. By 1880, electric trolleys had replaced horse-drawn carriages on New York streets.

Always fascinated by inventions, Barnum kept up with the times. He was the first to advertise with huge illuminated billboards. He also imported waterproof canvas from France for his Big Top.

twice a day. No one missed the spectacle. Even Queen Victoria and the Prince of Wales attended. The one-hundred-day run was an astounding success.

Final Curtain

After returning from London, Barnum, his family, and two hundred guests celebrated his eightieth birthday on July 5, 1890. In November of the same year, Barnum suffered a stroke and was confined to his home. Knowing his days were numbered, the circus

man used the time to update his autobiography and make certain his will was in order. Barnum also wondered what newspapers would say about him when he was gone. Learning of this, *The Evening Sun,* a New York City newspaper, published Barnum's obituary in advance, so that he might enjoy it. On March 24, 1891, Barnum opened the paper and read:

> Great and Only Barnum. He Wanted To Read His Obituary; Here It Is. Mr. Barnum has had almost everything in this life . . . and there is no reason why he should not have this last pleasure which he asks for. So here is the great showman's life, briefly and simply told, as it would have appeared in *The Evening Sun* had fate taken our Great and Only from us. It will be read with as great interest by the public as by Mr. Barnum.[7]

This introduction was followed by four columns of biographical information and was illustrated with woodcuts of Barnum at his present age, at the age of

From Prince of Humbugs to Children's Friend

As Barnum grew older he preferred to think of himself as the "grand entertainer to the world's children."[8] He loved and spoiled his own grandchildren and great-grandchildren and donated generously to Bridgeport's Boys' and Girls' Clubs and to an orphan asylum. In 1890, Barnum requested that the caption under his picture on circus posters read: THE CHILDREN'S FRIEND.

In later years, Barnum did not wish to be remembered as a humbug, but as a friend to children.

A King's Ransom

It was a common practice in the late nineteenth century to hold a body for ransom. Seven weeks after Barnum's burial, an attempt was made to steal his body from the vault in Mountain Grove.[9] The showman would have been pleased to know he made news even after he had been buried.

forty-one, of his mother, of Charity, and of Jenny Lind.

The real event followed shortly. On April 5, 1891, Nancy recorded that "death was kind. No physical pain disturbed the quiet figure on the little bed."[10] Phineas Taylor Barnum passed quietly away at 6:34 in the evening. He was buried in Bridgeport's Mountain Grove Cemetery. His grave is marked by a small headstone engraved with a phrase Barnum loved: "Not my will, but thine, be done." The Boston *Herald* newspaper proclaimed him "the foremost showman of all time."[11] Barnum had outlived the ridicule and bias against him.

With Barnum gone, Nancy moved to France. She married twice more, but of all her husbands, Nancy always remembered Barnum with great affection and respect.

11

THE WORLD'S GREATEST SHOWMAN

By the end of his life, Barnum could claim an amazing assortment of careers. He had been a lottery salesman, a best-selling author, a mayor, a manager, a publisher, a public speaker, and the owner of one of America's biggest and most successful museums and circuses.

It is the sum of all these experiences that illustrates Barnum's true talent. He was more than a promoter of oddities or circus acts. He was a shrewd businessman with a creative marketing mind. Even as a young man, Barnum used imaginative advertising techniques. With colorful animal murals, a rooftop spotlight, and a pavement-pounding bricklayer, Barnum drew the public's attention to his American Museum.

The site of Barnum's final resting place in Bridgeport's Mountain Grove Cemetery is marked by this monument.

Barnum and Twain

Mark Twain became a fan of the showman's career after reading Barnum's autobiography, probably the 1869 edition. Though Twain thought little of the showman as a political candidate, the two gentlemen eventually became friends. In 1874, Twain penned an ad selling passenger seats on the tail of a comet. In the ad, he encouraged people to contact Barnum for tickets.[1]

Barnum said, "I believe hugely in advertising and blowing my own trumpet, beating the gongs, drums, etc., to attract attention to a show. . . . "[2] This technique made the names Jenny Lind and Jumbo part of every American's vocabulary for years after.

Even in his own time, the public recognized Barnum's marketing skills. He received hundreds of letters asking him to promote three-legged chickens with two rectums and other oddities. Many requests were so entertaining that Barnum and his friend Mark Twain agreed to co-author a book filled with the wild letters.[3] Unfortunately, this project was never completed.

Even today, entrepreneurs can learn from the bold techniques of P. T. Barnum. A book published in 1998, *There's a Customer Born Every Minute: P. T. Barnum's Secrets to Business Success* by Joe Vitale, analyzes ways the showman successfully marketed his businesses and himself. In fact, Barnum's name was so well-known that a letter mailed from New Zealand and addressed only to "Mr. Barnum, America" was delivered without delay.

Zest for Life

In the 1840s, when American society preached that leisure time should be spent in constructive, educational activities, Barnum believed that "amusement [gave] zest to life and [made] a grand improvement in human character."[4] With his American Museum, the showman set out to change the general public's attitudes toward entertainment.

To accomplish this, Barnum collected an extraordinary variety of exhibits, placed them under one roof, and then stressed the educational value of a museum visit. In truth, most artifacts were displayed for their drawing power, not what could be learned from them. However, this marketing ploy, along with the cheap tickets that provided customers with hours of pleasure, established museums as family recreation centers.

After convincing the public that museums offered educational opportunity, Barnum tackled an even bigger challenge—making plays acceptable to the general public. He lived up to his promise that nothing offensive would be shown or uttered there. He presented plays such as *The Drunkard* devised both to entertain and to provide an uplifting lesson. After each showing of this particular play, the audience was urged to go to the box office and sign the teetotaler pledge. With this kind of carefully staged melodrama or comedy,

A Generous Man

In his final years, the showman collected about one hundred fifty thousand dollars annually from the circus and owned real estate worth $4 million. Barnum did not keep all this wealth for himself. He was a philanthropist who contributed generously to the Bridgeport Public Library, the Bridgeport Hospital, the city's Seaside Park, the Actor's Fund of America, and the Universalist Church. He also donated fifty thousand dollars to Tufts College in Medford, Massachusetts, for the Barnum Museum of Natural History, and later donated Jumbo's stuffed hide. Tufts adopted Jumbo as the name of the school's football team. Today, Barnum Hall, which stands on the site of the museum that burned in 1875, and the Jumbo mascot preserve the memory of P. T. Barnum on the Tufts University campus.

Barnum made the theater an acceptable diversion for American families.

Greatest Show on Earth

Phineas Taylor Barnum is still remembered for one of his final accomplishments—his circus—best described as the Greatest Show on Earth. The Greatest Show on Earth operated during the heyday of the American circus that began in the 1870s when large circuses began traveling by rail. It lasted for fifty years. Barnum's gifts to the circus included the addition of grandeur and

Colorful Conversation

Barnum is well remembered for his colorful conversation. The best-known comment credited to him is: "There's a sucker born every minute." However, the word *sucker* was not used as a slang term during Barnum's lifetime and no record has ever been found that he actually spoke these words. It is doubtful that the showman would have made such a statement. Barnum truly believed that he almost always gave the public what they wanted and more.

We can thank Barnum's circus, however, for several other colorful words and phrases now commonly used in American English. *Jumbo* now means the biggest size or kind. *Throwing your hat in the ring* was coined when a local politician declared his intention to run for office by throwing his hat into Barnum and Bailey's circus ring. *Let's get the show on the road*, the cry heard when it was time to load the circus animals on the train, now means it is time to get going.

an astonishing variety that created a show that was larger-than-life.

He also embellished the traditional circus parade. When the elephants, caged animals, clowns, acrobats, horse-drawn calliope, and beautifully carved wagons rolled through town, everyone took a holiday to watch. Barnum made a day at the circus every child's

Sideshow stars Anna Swan and Captain Bates—giants who stood seven feet eleven inches tall—tower over an average-sized man. Barnum is still remembered for the unusual people he employed in his exhibitions.

dream. He also created many souvenirs to be sold at the circus. Some of these were children's books that Barnum wrote about his circus animals. The most popular story, published in 1876, was called *Lion Jack: A Story of Perilous Adventures Among Wild Men and the Capturing of Wild Beasts, Showing How Menageries Are Made.*

Knowing that living curiosities drew large crowds, Barnum added the sideshow—an elaborate show within a show—to his circus. While these "freak shows," as they were called then, may seem cruel today, Barnum called these living curiosities the "representatives of the wonderful."[5] He valued the people in his exhibits, treated them fairly, and paid them good wages. Among his crowd pleasers were giant men and women standing more than seven feet tall, midgets, albino children, bearded ladies, and tattooed men.

Barnum introduced the three-ring circus, an idea that became so popular that competing circuses were forced to add another ring. By 1891, there were seven large circuses touring the country by rail. Barnum's was the largest. It took sixty-five railroad cars to move from town to town. The smallest circus, the Ringling Brothers' show, needed only twenty.

Without a doubt, the showman saved his best act for last. Though Phineas Taylor Barnum has been gone for more than one hundred years, his spirit, his memory, and his name live on today as part of the Ringling Brothers' and Barnum and Bailey Circus—still known as the Greatest Show on Earth.

CHRONOLOGY

1810—*July 5*: Born in Bethel, Connecticut.

1816—Starts school in Bethel.

1818—Begins to work in his father's country store.

1825—*September 7*: Taylor's father, Philo Barnum, dies.

1826—Works in grocery in New York City; Runs his own saloon.

1828—Moves back to Bethel; Opens the Yellow Store and operates lotteries.

1829—*November 8*: Marries Charity Hallett.

1831—Publishes *The Herald of Freedom* newspaper.

1833—*May 27*: Caroline Cordelia, his first daughter, is born; Barnum moves his family to New York City.

1835—Exhibits Joice Heth.

1836—Moves family to Bethel; Tours with Turner's Old Columbian Circus.

1841—Moves back to New York; Purchases the American Museum collection.

April 18: Helen, his second daughter, is born.

1842—Promotes the Fejee Mermaid; Discovers Charles Stratton, better known as Tom Thumb.

1844—Tom Thumb tour goes to England; Command performance for Queen Victoria.

April 11: Frances, his third daughter, is born.

1846—*March 1*: Pauline, his fourth daughter, is born; Daughter Frances dies shortly before her second birthday.

1848—Joins the temperance movement; Moves into his first and most elaborate mansion, Iranistan.

1850—Promotes the Jenny Lind tour.

1854—Writes his autobiography, *The Life of P. T. Barnum, Written by Himself*.

1855—Sells the American Museum collection and retires.

1856—Declares bankruptcy following the Jerome Clock scandal; Sets off with Tom Thumb on a new European tour.

1858—Makes his debut as a public lecturer.

1860—Repays all his debts and repurchases the American Museum.

1865—Elected to the Connecticut state legislature.

July 13: Fire destroys the American Museum; New museum opens in September.

1867—Defeated in his run for a seat in the United States Congress.

1868—*March 3*: The New American Museum burns.

Barnum quits museum business; Barnum's mother, Irena, dies.

1869—Moves into new home, Waldemere; Travels with English friend, John Fish.

1871—Begins career as a circus promoter when Barnum's Grand Traveling Museum, Menagerie, Caravan, and Circus opens.

1873—*November 20*: Wife Charity dies while Barnum is in Europe.

1874—*February 14*: Secretly marries Nancy Fish.

September 16: Couple remarries in New York. The Great Roman Hippodrome opens in April.

1875—Elected mayor of Bridgeport.

1880—Signs partnership with Bailey and Cooper, owners of the Great London Circus.

1887—Barnum and Bailey form second partnership, without Cooper, and promote the Barnum and Bailey Greatest Show on Earth.

1882—Purchases his greatest attraction, Jumbo.

1885—*September 15*: Jumbo struck by train and killed.

1889—Takes the Greatest Show on Earth to London.

1891—*March 24*: Enjoys reading his own obituary.

April 5: Barnum dies at the age of eighty.

CHAPTER NOTES

Chapter 1. Barnum's Jumbo Attraction

1. P. T. Barnum, *Struggles and Triumphs: Forty Years' Recollections of P. T. Barnum* (Buffalo: The Courier Company, 1883), p. 332.

2. Philip B. Kunhardt, Jr., Philip B. Kunhardt III, and Peter W. Kunhardt, *P. T. Barnum: America's Greatest Showman* (New York: Knopf, 1995), p. 278.

3. Neil Harris, *Humbug, The Art of P. T. Barnum* (Boston: Little, Brown and Company,1973), p. 257.

4. Barnum, p. 333.

5. P. T. Barnum, *Barnum's Own Story*, ed. Waldo R. Browne (Gloucester: Peter Smith, 1972), p. 431.

6. Harris, p. 257.

7. Kunhardt et al., p. 280.

8. Ibid., p. 298.

9. Harris, p. 265.

Chapter 2. Birth of a Humbug

1. Irving Wallace, *The Fabulous Showman, The Life and Times of P. T. Barnum* (New York: Alfred A. Knopf, 1959), p. 26.

2. A. H. Saxon, *P. T. Barnum, the Legend and the Man* (New York: Columbia University Press, 1989), p. 28.

3. P. T. Barnum, *Struggles and Triumphs: Forty Years' Recollections of P. T. Barnum* (Buffalo: The Courier Company, 1883), p.19.

4. P. T. Barnum, *Barnum's Own Story*, ed. Waldo R. Browne (Gloucester: Peter Smith, 1972), pp. 17–18.

5. Ibid., p. 18.

6. Wallace, p. 27.

7. Barnum, *Barnum's Own Story*, p. 5.

8. Barnum, *Struggles and Triumphs*, p. 17.

9. Barnum, *Barnum's Own Story*, p. 5.

10. Neil Harris, *Humbug, The Art of P. T. Barnum* (Boston: Little, Brown and Company,1973), p. 11.

11. Wallace, pp. 31–32.

12. Saxon, p. 33.

13. Ibid.

Chapter 3. Tricks of the Trade

1. P. T. Barnum, *Barnum's Own Story*, ed. Waldo R. Browne (Gloucester: Peter Smith, 1972), p. 23.

2. Ibid., p 24.

3. P. T. Barnum, *Struggles and Triumphs: Forty Years' Recollections of P. T. Barnum* (Buffalo: The Courier Company, 1883), p. 24.

4. Ibid., p. 32.

5. Ibid., p. 33.

6. Ibid.

7. Philip B. Kunhardt, Jr., Philip B. Kunhardt III, and Peter W. Kunhardt, *P. T. Barnum: America's Greatest Showman* (New York: Knopf, 1995), p.16.

8. Neil Harris, *Humbug, The Art of P. T. Barnum* (Boston: Little, Brown and Company, 1973), p. 20.

9. Ibid., p. 21.

10. Kunhardt et al., p. 20.

11. Ibid.

12. Ibid., p. 22.

13. Ibid.

14. Barnum, *Struggles and Triumphs*, p. 39.

15. Irving Wallace, *The Fabulous Showman, The Life and Times of P. T. Barnum* (New York: Alfred A. Knopf, 1959), p. 40.

Chapter 4. The American Museum

1. P. T. Barnum, *Struggles and Triumphs: Forty Years' Recollections of P. T. Barnum* (Buffalo: The Courier Company, 1883), p. 52.

2. Ibid., p. 56.

3. Neil Harris, *Humbug, The Art of P. T. Barnum* (Boston: Little, Brown and Company,1973), p. 56.

4. A. H. Saxon, *P. T. Barnum, the Legend and the Man* (New York: Columbia University Press, 1989), p. 1.

5. Barnum, p. 47.

6. Andrea Stulman Dennett, *Weird & Wonderful, The Dime Museum in America* (New York: New York University Press, 1997), p. 32.

7. Philip B. Kunhardt, Jr., Philip B. Kunhardt III, and Peter W. Kunhardt, *P. T. Barnum: America's Greatest Showman* (New York: Knopf, 1995), p. 43.

8. Ibid., p. 46.

9. P. T. Barnum, *Barnum's Own Story*, ed. Waldo R. Browne (Gloucester: Peter Smith, 1972), pp. 121–122.

10. Barnum, *Struggles and Triumphs*, p. 62.

Chapter 5. General Tom Thumb

1. P. T. Barnum, *Barnum's Own Story*, ed. Waldo R. Browne (Gloucester: Peter Smith, 1972), p. 133.

2. A. H. Saxon, *P. T. Barnum, the Legend and the Man* (New York: Columbia University Press, 1989), p. 123.

3. Irving Wallace, *The Fabulous Showman, The Life and Times of P. T. Barnum* (New York: Alfred A. Knopf, 1959), p. 73.

4. Raymond Fitzsimons, *Barnum in London* (London: Geoffrey Bles, 1969), p. 60.

5. Wallace, pp.73–74.

6. Saxon, p. 126.

7. Wallace, p. 76.

8. Saxon, p. 129.

9. Ibid.

10. Ibid.

11. Fitzsimons, p. 66.

12. Neil Harris, *Humbug, The Art of P. T. Barnum* (Boston: Little, Brown and Company, 1973), pp. 94–95.

13. Ibid., p. 95.

14. P. T. Barnum, *Struggles and Triumphs: Forty Years' Recollections of P. T. Barnum* (Buffalo: The Courier Company, 1883), p. 75.

15. Ibid., p. 76.

16. Ibid.

17. Wallace, p. 83.

18. Saxon, p. 136.

Chapter 6. Husband and Father

1. Philip B. Kunhardt, Jr., Philip B. Kunhardt III, and Peter W. Kunhardt, *P. T. Barnum: America's Greatest Showman* (New York: Knopf, 1995), p. 79.

2. Ibid.

3. Ibid., p. 69.

4. Ibid., p. 68.

5. A. H. Saxon, *P. T. Barnum, the Legend and the Man* (New York: Columbia University Press, 1989), p. 151.

6. Ibid.

7. Ibid., p. 84.

8. P. T. Barnum, *Struggles and Triumphs: Forty Years' Recollections of P. T. Barnum* (Buffalo: The Courier Company, 1883), p. 99.

Chapter 7. Respect for a Humbug

1. Philip B. Kunhardt, Jr., Philip B. Kunhardt III, and Peter W. Kunhardt, *P. T. Barnum: America's Greatest Showman* (New York: Knopf, 1995), p. 105.

2. P. T. Barnum, *Barnum's Own Story*, ed. Waldo R. Browne (Gloucester: Peter Smith, 1972), p. 192.

3. Irving Wallace, *The Fabulous Showman, The Life and Times of P. T. Barnum* (New York: Alfred A. Knopf, 1959), p. 123.

4. P. T. Barnum, *Struggles and Triumphs: Forty Years' Recollections of P. T. Barnum* (Buffalo: The Courier Company, 1883), p. 105.

5. Wallace, pp. 131–132.

6. Neil Harris, *Humbug, The Art of P. T. Barnum* (Boston: Little, Brown and Company,1973), p. 207.

7. Wallace, p. 168.

8. Ibid., p. 182.

9. Kunhardt et al., p. 125.

10. Barnum, *Struggles and Triumphs*, p. 149.

11. Ibid., p. 166.

12. Ibid., p. 168.

Chapter 8. Rebuilding Dreams

1. Neil Harris, *Humbug, The Art of P. T. Barnum* (Boston: Little, Brown and Company,1973), p. 165.

2. Ibid., p. 167.

3. Philip B. Kunhardt, Jr., Philip B. Kunhardt III, and Peter W. Kunhardt, *P. T. Barnum: America's Greatest Showman* (New York: Knopf, 1995), p. 142.

4. Irving Wallace, *The Fabulous Showman, The Life and Times of P. T. Barnum* (New York: Alfred A. Knopf, 1959), p. 186.

5. Ibid., p. 187.

6. P. T. Barnum, *Struggles and Triumphs: Forty Years' Recollections of P. T. Barnum* (Buffalo: The Courier Company, 1883), p. 241.

7. Ibid., p. 245.

8. Harris, p. 190.

9. Barnum, p. 266.

Chapter 9. Under the Big Top

1. P. T. Barnum, *Struggles and Triumphs: Forty Years' Recollections of P. T. Barnum* (Buffalo: The Courier Company, 1883), p. 281.

2. Ibid.

3. Philip B. Kunhardt, Jr., Philip B. Kunhardt III, and Peter W. Kunhardt, *P. T. Barnum: America's Greatest Showman* (New York: Knopf, 1995), p. 220.

4. Barnum, p. 283.

5. Kunhardt et al., pp. 242–243.

6. Ibid., p. 239.

7. Ibid., p. 240.

8. Ibid., p. 247.

Chapter 10. The Greatest Show on Earth

1. Philip B. Kunhardt, Jr., Philip B. Kunhardt III, and Peter W. Kunhardt, *P. T. Barnum: America's Greatest Showman* (New York: Knopf, 1995), p. 272.

2. P. T. Barnum, *Barnum's Own Story*, ed. Waldo R. Browne (Gloucester: Peter Smith, 1972), p. 424.

3. Irving Wallace, *The Fabulous Showman, The Life and Times of P. T. Barnum* (New York: Alfred A. Knopf, 1959) p. 240.

4. Ibid., p. 242.

5. A. H. Saxton, *P. T. Barnum: The Legend and the Man* (New York: Columbia University Press, 1989), p. 282.

6. Kunhardt et al., p. 269.

7. Wallace, p. 252.

8. Kunhardt et al., p. 330.

9. Neil Harris, *Humbug, The Art of P. T. Barnum* (Boston: Little, Brown and Company,1973), p. 279.

10. Kunhardt et al., p. 344.

11. Ibid., p. 344.

Chapter 11. The World's Greatest Showman

1. Joe Vitale, *There's a Customer Born Every Minute* (New York: American Management Association, 1998), p. 19.

2. Ibid., p. 16.

3. Ibid., p. 122.

4. Philip B. Kunhardt, Jr., Philip B. Kunhardt III, and Peter W. Kunhardt, *P. T. Barnum: America's Greatest Showman* (New York: Knopf, 1995), p. ix.

5. Ibid., p. 234.

GLOSSARY

Big Top—The main tent of the circus that held the performance rings.

capital—Wealth, money, or property used in business.

collateral—Stocks, bonds, or property used to guarantee a loan.

doctrine—Principles of a religion.

entrepreneur—A person who organizes and manages a business, taking a risk for the sake of making a profit.

four-pence—British currency worth six cents.

gilding—The art of applying gold leaf, or gold covering, to a surface.

Hippodrome—In ancient Greece or Rome, a course for chariot and horse races; an arena or building for a circus.

hoaxes and ruses—Tricks or fraud.

lithograph—A print made through a process in which a metal plate was used to reproduce photographs.

menagerie—A collection of animals.

merchandizing—Advertising, promoting, and organizing the sale of a particular product.

steerage—Formerly a section in some ships, with the poorest accommodations, occupied by the passengers paying the lowest fares.

stock—Capital investment in a company through the purchase of shares, usually entitling the owners to interest, dividends, and voting rights.

taxidermist—One who stuffs and mounts the skins of animals, making them appear lifelike.

temperance—The belief that liquor should not be consumed or sold. In the nineteenth century, strong alcohol such as rum and whiskey were considered liquor, though wine and hard cider generally were not.

FURTHER READING

Andronik, Cathy. *Prince of Humbugs: The Life of P. T. Barnum*. Old Tappan, N.J.: Macmillan, 1994.

Duncan, Lois. *The Circus Comes Home: When the Greatest Show on Earth Rode the Rails*. New York: Doubleday Books for Young Readers, 1993.

Pflueger, Lynda. *Mark Twain: Legendary Writer and Humorist*. Berkeley Heights, N.J.: Enslow Publishers, Inc.,1999.

Presnall, Judith J. *Circuses: Under the Big Top*. Danbury, Conn.: Franklin Watts, 1996.

Wright, David K. *P. T. Barnum*. New York: Raintree Steck-Vaughn, 1997.

INTERNET ADDRESSES

The Barnum Museum. n.d. <http://38.148.190.165>.

Ringling Bros. and Barnum & Bailey Online. 2000. <http://www.ringling.com/home.asp>.

INDEX

A

Aaron Turner's Old Columbian
    Circus, 32
abolition movement, 26, 29–30,
    63–64, 80
Adelaide, dowager queen of
    England, 51
American Museum, 34–36,
    37–40, 41, 42, 44, 46, 47,
    51, 53, 54, 56, 63, 69, 73,
    74, 75–77, 79, 82, 83–85, 86,
    89, 108, 111
American Society for the
    Prevention of Cruelty to
    Animals (ASPCA), 102, 103
Art of Money-Getting, The, 74, 87

B

Bailey, George, 95
Bailey, James A., 99, 103, 113
Barnum, Almira (sister), 14
Barnum, Caroline Cordelia
    (daughter), 28, 32, 35, 55,
    56, 58, 70, 92–93
Barnum, Charity Hallett (first
    wife), 25–26, 29–30, 32, 35,
    55–56, 58, 59, 69, 70, 73,
    85, 86, 92, 107
Barnum, Cordelia (sister), 14
Barnum, Eder (brother), 14
Barnum, Frances (daughter), 55,
    56
Barnum, Helen (daughter), 35,
    55, 56, 70–72, 73, 92–93
Barnum, Irena Taylor (mother),
    14, 15, 17, 22, 26, 85, 107
Barnum, Mary (sister), 14
Barnum, Nancy Fish (second
    wife), 87, 92–93, 94, 103,
    107
Barnum, Pauline (daughter), 56,
    72, 92–93

Barnum, Philo (father), 14, 15,
    17, 20, 21, 22
Barnum, Philo (half brother), 42
Barnum, Phineas Taylor
    advertising, 37, 43–44, 66,
        69, 104, 108
    birth, 14
    buys American Museum,
        34–35, 74
    childhood, 19–21, 22
    circus owner, 5, 6–13,
        87–88, 89–90, 92,
        93–95, 97, 101–102,
        103–104, 108
    cruelty charges, 101–102,
        103
    daily routine, 61–62
    death, 107
    drinking, 56, 58–59
    education, 20
    fires, 73–74, 79, 82,
        83–85, 86, 90
    first marriage, 26
    Jenny Lind tour, 64–69
    Jerome Clock scandal, 72,
        73–74
    lecturer, 74, 96
    legacy, 108, 110–115
    lotteries, 23–24, 25, 28, 108
    newspaper, 28, 29
    patriotism, 78–82
    politician, 80–82, 84, 95,
        96, 97, 108
    religion, 18–19
    second marriage, 92–93
    three-ring circus, 99–101,
        115
    travels, 51–53, 55–56, 60,
        74, 86–87, 103–104
    writer, 28, 69, 70, 82, 105,
        108, 115

Barnum's and London 7 United Monster Shows, 5, 9–10, 99–101

Barnum's Grand Scientific and Musical Theater, 32

Barnum's Traveling World's Fair, 90

Barnum, Taylor (brother), 14

Bell, Alexander Graham, 104

Bergh, Henry, 102, 103

Bethel, Connecticut, 14, 18, 19, 23, 25–28, 32

Bonaparte, Napoleon, 44, 55

Booth, John Wilkes, 82

Boston Museum, 37, 38

brick layer, 37–38, 108

Bridgeport, Connecticut, 59, 72, 78, 95, 96, 97, 105, 107, 112

Bump, Mercy Lavinia Warren, 46, 80

C

Chapin, Edwin, 58–59

Civil War, 63, 77, 78–82

Compromise of 1850, 63–64

Confederate States of America, 77

Congregational Church, 18–19

Connecticut state legislature, 15, 28, 80–82, 84

Cooper, James E., 99

Costello, Don, 87, 95, 97

Coup, William Cameron, 87, 88, 89, 95, 97

Cushman, Pauline, 80

D

Donaldson, W. H., 93

E

East Bridgeport, Connecticut, 72

Edison, Thomas Alva, 104

Edward VII, 48, 77, 104

Egyptian Hall, 48, 49

Everett, Edward, 48

F

Fairchild, Polly, 14

Fejee Mermaid, 38–40, 41

Fish, John, 86–87, 92

Fish, Nancy. *See* Barnum, Nancy Fish.

Frost, Hyatt, 32

G

Gerry, Elbridge T., 101–102

Greatest Show on Earth, 97, 99, 103–104, 112–115

Great London Circus, 98–99

Greenwood, John Jr., 69

Griffin, J., 39

H

Hallett, Charity. *See* Barnum, Charity Hallett.

Hendershot, Robert, 79–80

Herald of Freedom, The, 28, 29

Heth, Joice, 29–32

Howes, Seth B., 89

Hund, Samuel H., 73

I

Iranistan, 60, 61, 69, 73–74, 75

Ivy Island, 16–18, 34–35

J

Jerome Clock Company, 72, 73–74

John Scudder's American Museum. *See* American Museum.

Jumbo, 5, 6–13, 101, 103, 110, 112, 113

June, Lewis, 95

K

Kennedy, Robert C., 79

Kimball, Moses, 37, 38–39

L

Lee, Robert E., 82

Life of P. T. Barnum, Written by Himself, 69, 70, 82, 110

Lincoln, Abraham, 77, 80, 82

Lindencroft, 75, 85

Lind, Jenny, 64–69, 107, 110

London Zoo, 5, 6, 8, 11, 13, 101

Louis Philippe, king of France, 55

Lyceum Bureau, 96
Lyman, Levi, 30, 39

M
Madison Square Garden, 9, 99
Mountain Grove Cemetery, 107

N
Nathans, John, 95
New American Museum. *See* American Museum.
New York, 9, 24, 26, 29, 30, 33–34, 38, 40, 43, 53, 59, 66, 67, 73, 76, 79, 80, 87, 90, 92, 93, 99, 101, 102, 104
New York Museum Company, 35
Nutt, George Washington Morrison, 80

O
Olmsted, Francis, 34–35, 37, 41

P
Parliament, 7–8
Prince of Wales. *See* Edward VII.
Prudential Committee, 78
P. T. Barnum's Advance Courier, 94–95
P. T. Barnum's Grand Traveling Museum, Menagerie, Caravan, and Circus, 88
P. T. Barnum's Greatest Show on Earth, 97
P. T. Barnum's Great Traveling Exposition and World's Fair, 90

R
Redpath, James, 96
Republican party, 77, 80, 84, 95
Ringling Brothers' and Barnum and Bailey Circus. *See* Greatest Show on Earth.
Royal Zoological Gardens. *See* London Zoo.

S
Scott, Matthew, 6, 8–9, 10–11, 101

Sherman, H. G., 50, 51, 54
Smith, Avery, 95
Society for the Prevention of Cruelty to Children, 101–102
Stowe, Harriet Beecher, 64, 96
Stratton, Charles Sherwood. *See* Thumb, Tom.
Stratton, Cynthia, 42, 43, 46, 47, 49
Stratton, Sherwood, 42, 43, 46, 49
Struggles and Triumphs, 70
Swan, Anna, 82

T
Taylor, Phineas (grandfather), 15–18, 19–20, 25, 35
temperance movement, 58–59, 96, 111
Thompson, David, 70
Thumb, Tom, 42–46, 47, 48–50, 51, 54, 55, 58, 60, 73, 74, 80, 87
Turner, Aaron, 89
Twain, Mark, 69, 84, 96, 110

U
Uncle Tom's Cabin, 64
Unitarian Church, 26
United States Congress, 63–64, 84, 95
Universalist Church, 19, 112

V
Victoria, queen of England, 7–8, 48, 49, 104

W
Waldemere, 85, 92–93
Ward, Henry A., 11–12
Washington, Augustine, 29
Washington, D.C., 64, 67, 80
Washington, George, 29, 38
Wilton, John Hall, 64

Y
Yellow Store, 25, 26–28, 29